Innkeepers' Best

Quick Breads

60 Delicious Recipes Shared by
Bed & Breakfast Innkeepers
Across the Country

Laura Zahn

Down to Earth Publications

Published by
Down to Earth Publications
1032 West Montana Avenue
St. Paul, MN 55117

Library of Congress Cataloging in Publication Data

Zahn, Laura C., 1957 -
    Innkeepers' best quick breads/Laura C. Zahn
    p.   cm.
    Includes index.
    ISBN 0-99939301-99-7
    1. Breakfasts 2. Breads 3. Bed and breakfast accommodations - U.S. - directories
    TX770.M83
Dewey System - Ideas for Breakfast and Brunch - 651.52
Printed in the USA
99 00 01 02 03 5 4 3 2 1

Cover photo: Lemon Verbena Bread (see recipe, page 81) courtesy of the Inn at Cedar Crossing, Sturgeon Bay, Wisconsin, photo by Bill Paulson, Stevens Point, Wisconsin.

Cover and interior design by Helene C. J. Anderson, Stillwater, Minnesota

To order additional copies by mail, send a check or money order for $12.95 each to Down to Earth Publications, 1032 W. Montana Ave., St. Paul, MN 55117 (includes shipping by 4th class mail). If you wish UPS delivery, send a check for $13.95 and include a street address (no P.O. boxes). To charge your order with a Visa or MasterCard, call 800-585-6211 or fax 651-488-7862.

Introduction

*Q*uick breads. Bed & Breakfast innkeepers have perfected the art of this sweet, yet hearty and satisfying, accompaniment to breakfast — or tea time, or snack time! Most of the bread recipes in here are truly sweet! (Don't be afraid to try the savory ones, too!) And all of them are quick — requiring no yeast, that needs to rise, punch down, and rise again. They're usually quick to whip up and pop in the oven, as well.

And all of them are Innkeepers' Best — they have won rave reviews from B&B guests who may have asked the innkeepers for the recipes or requested a particular bread be made on return visits.

Many of the recipes are favorites not just of guests, but of innkeepers too. Busy innkeepers might double recipes and freeze extra loaves — in many cases, these are moist breads, usually served cold or at room temperature, and so they hold their moisture when thawing and still taste wonderful.

Whether you are looking for some new ideas to serve your family, for bake sale or potluck contributions, or for something to package nicely and give away on special occasions, this is the collection for you.

Traditional favorites, such as banana bread, have been included, as well as those with delicious twists — such as adding bits of dried apricots, like it's made at the Graham B&B Inn and Adobe Village in Sedona, Arizona. Other popular breads, like lemon, pumpkin, cranberry-orange or zucchini, have been elevated to new heights by innovative innkeepers.

And then there are new creations, like a moist pumpkin bread infused with chocolate-covered raisins from Justin Trails in Sparta, Wisconsin, or the Chocolate Pepper Pound Cake from Doanleigh Inn in Kansas City, Missouri.

Whether it's made in a "regular" bread loaf pan, a Bundt pan or miniature loaf pans, it's bound to be delicious if it came from these veteran innkeepers, whose food must pass a taste test every single morning. (By the way, if you haven't invested in insulated baking pans, do so now; they are definitely worth it! And try mini-loaf pans. Just remember to cut the baking time. Also, be sure to use unbleached flour and large eggs in these recipes.)

And if the recipe makes a bit too much for you and yours to enjoy, consider giving away a loaf to a friend or neighbor. Please continue the tradition of hospitality practiced by these innkeepers, and share the best of your kitchen with others. It'll brighten someone else's day — and yours, too!

"Inn-joy!"

– Laura Zahn

CONTENTS

Quick Bread Recipes ■ 7 to 125

Cleburne House

*T*his beautifully restored Queen Anne-style Victorian was built in 1886. Vestiges of its heritage are evident its twelve-foot ceilings, massive pocket doors, stained glass windows, and wraparound veranda with gingerbread trim. Innkeeper Jan Bills, who searched high and low across Texas before discovering this Victorian home, has filled the house with her antique doll and furniture collection.

The four guestrooms are located on the second floor, and two of them have access to a screened porch. Jan completely redecorated the house in 1997 with new wallpaper, paint and draperies. Because she loves to garden, she tilled all the garden surrounding the house to recondition the soil for beautiful flowers. The Inn has been the site of many weddings over the past two years.

Cleburne House's magnificent gardens contain crepe myrtle, Carolina jasmine, large oaks, flower shrubs, herbs, and roses. Visitors linger on the wide veranda, enjoying tea and homemade cookies and ice cream and watching wild birds and hummingbirds flit among nearby feeders.

Cleburne House is within walking distance of the historic Johnson County Courthouse, Andrew Carnegie Library, Layland Museum, and many interesting antique shops. Also nearby are golf courses, canoeing, boutiques, Pat Cleburne State Park, and Texas Wildlife Safari. After a busy day, guests love to relax in the front parlor, where they're welcome to play Jan's grandmother's piano, read, or play board games. Learn more on the Web, www.digitex.net/cleburnehouse/

Cleburne House

201 N. Anglin
Cleburne, TX 76031
817-641-0085

Almond Poppyseed Bread

"This recipe was given to me by an accountant, Micki Long, with whom I worked in Des Moines, Iowa, in the 1980s," said Jan Bills, innkeeper. "At one time, I had purchased baking molds of Christmas trees, and this recipe makes 30 little tree cakes. Then I drizzle powdered sugar icing on the little trees. If you make little decorative molds with this recipe, you will only want to bake them 16 or 17 minutes." Makes 2 loaves.

   3 cups flour
2½ cups sugar
1½ teaspoons baking powder
1½ teaspoons salt
   3 eggs
1½ cups milk
1⅛ cups vegetable oil
1½ tablespoons poppyseed
1½ teaspoons vanilla extract
1½ teaspoons almond extract
1½ teaspoons butter flavoring

Glaze
¾ cup sugar
¼ cup orange juice
½ teaspoon almond extract
½ teaspoon vanilla extract
½ teaspoon butter flavoring

- Preheat oven to 350 degrees. Grease 2 9 x 5-inch loaf pans.
- In a large bowl, place all bread ingredients. Beat with electric mixer for 2 minutes at medium speed.
- Pour into loaf pans. Bake the loaves for 1 hour or until a knife inserted in the center comes out clean.
- For the glaze, mix together the sugar, orange juice, almond extract, vanilla extract, and butter flavoring. Brush onto the loaves while still warm. Let cool before removing from pans and slicing.

Whitefish Bay Farm
Bed & Breakfast

*T*his restored 1908 American Foursquare farmhouse has been open as a bed and breakfast since 1991. Innkeepers Dick and Gretchen Regnery run a working farm here as well, raising tranquil Corriedale sheep and famous Door County cherries.

The names of Whitefish Bay Farm's guestrooms evoke the delightful flowers that dot nearby meadows and orchards each spring: Buttercup Room; Trillium Room; Apple Blossom Room; Iris Room. After a peaceful night surrounded by a charming assortment of quilts, handwoven wool rugs and throws, and original art, guests are greeted each morning with an abundant from-scratch breakfast in the Scandinavian-style dining room.

A visit to the B&B's art gallery in the granary barn is a must; a unique collection of photos and fiber art is on display here from Memorial Day weekend until mid-October. Weaving and hand spinning take place daily, using wool from the Regnery's own sheep.

The farm is located next to the rolling sand beaches of Whitefish Dunes State Park, near the popular — but secluded — sites of Clark Lake and Cave Point. Guests also have easy access to Door County's scenic backroad bicycle routes. Learn more on the Web, www.whitefishbayfarm.com

Whitefish Bay Farm B&B
3831 Clark Lake Road (County WD)
Sturgeon Bay, WI 54235
920-743-1560

Amaretto Cherry Bread

"This bread is best made with fresh cherries or with cherries that are snap frozen without a syrup," said Innkeeper Gretchen Regnery. "If you cannot find fresh or snap-frozen cherries, you can use frozen cherries in syrup. Be sure to thaw, drain, and rinse the frozen cherries before adding to the recipe, and decrease the amount of cherries to 1 cup." Makes 3 small loaves.

$1\frac{1}{2}$ cups flour
2 teaspoons baking powder
$\frac{1}{2}$ cup margarine
1 cup sugar
3 large eggs
$\frac{1}{2}$ cup almond-flavored liqueur, such as Amaretto
1 cup chopped pecans or walnuts or sliced almonds
$1\frac{1}{2}$ cup fresh or frozen red tart cherries
powdered sugar

- Preheat oven to 350 degrees. Spray 3 $3\frac{1}{4}$ x $5\frac{1}{2}$-inch loaf pans with non-stick cooking spray.
- In a medium bowl, sift together the flour and baking powder
- With an electric mixer, cream the sugar and margarine. Add the eggs, and beat until smooth.
- Add the flour mixture and the liqueur alternately to the egg mixture. Beat until smooth
- Stir in the cherries and nuts by hand. Divide batter evenly between pans.
- Bake for 40 to 50 minutes, or until a toothpick inserted in the middle comes out clean.
- Allow bread to cool in pan completely. To serve, sprinkle with powdered sugar before slicing.

Rose Manor Bed & Breakfast

*W*estern Lancaster County is a region of picturesque rolling farmland dotted with quaint villages. Rose Manor rests in a quiet residential neighborhood in the borough of Manheim, far from tour buses and crowds.

Rose Manor was built in 1905 by a local lumbermill owner and still contains its original chestnut woodwork and cabinetry. The decor is elegant and old-fashioned, somewhat Victorian, with comfortable chairs and sofas and antiques. An herbal theme is reflected in the names of the guestrooms, in decorative touches throughout the house, and in the cooking. The extensive herb gardens supply the perfect ingredients to make breakfast memorable. Tea is also served in the cozy tea room, by prior reservation.

When they began innkeeping in 1995, Susan Jenal and her mother, Anne, combined their love of cooking, pretty things, gardening, meeting new people, and hard work. Native New Yorkers, they've come to know the area better than some locals, yet they still see Lancaster through visitors' eyes and provide guests with a variety of suggestions on how to best enjoy their stay.

Area attractions and activities include Amish farms, the Pennsylvania Renaissance Faire, outlet shopping, Hershey, farmers markets, antiquing, the Strasburg Railroad, local historic sites and museums, bicycling, fishing and quilting. Rose Manor is also a convenient starting point for day trips to Gettysburg and Longwood Gardens.

Rose Manor Bed & Breakfast
124 South Linden Street
Manheim, PA 17545
717-664-4932
Fax 717-664-1611

Apple Cheddar Quick Bread

"This hearty bread is especially nice with an autumn brunch," said Innkeeper Susan Jenal. Makes 1 loaf.

> 2 cups self-rising flour
> ½ teaspoon cinnamon
> ⅔ cup sugar
> ½ cup coarsely broken pecans
> 2 eggs, slightly beaten
> ½ cup vegetable oil
> ½ cup shredded sharp Cheddar cheese
> ¼ cup milk
> 1½ cups peeled and finely chopped Granny Smith apples

- Preheat oven to 350 degrees. Liberally grease a 9 x 5-inch loaf pan.
- In a large bowl, combine the flour, cinnamon, sugar, and pecans.
- In another bowl, mix the eggs, vegetable oil, cheese, milk, and apples. Add to the flour mixture and stir just until blended (batter will be slightly lumpy).
- Spoon batter into pan and bake for 60 to 70 minutes, or until a toothpick inserted in the center comes out clean.
- Cool on a wire rack for about 15 minutes. Remove from pan and continue cooling on rack.

Lord Mayor's
Bed & Breakfast Inn

*T*his elegant Edwardian house was the home of the first mayor of Long Beach, Charles H. Windham. His unofficial Edwardian-style title, Lord Mayor, was bestowed by British beauty contestants enjoying the amenities of this seaside resort in the mid-1900s. The Lord Mayor's house was meticulously restored by historians Reuben and Laura Brasser and received the prestigious 1992 Great American Home Award from the National Trust for Historic Preservation for sensitivity in restoration of an historic house.

Their inn has expanded into a collection comprising a total of 12 rooms, with other rooms located in the Cinnamon House, the Apple House and the Garden House. The Garden House was converted from the original horse barn and the others are 1908 city cottages near the original mayor's home.

Located in the heart of Long Beach, Lord Mayor's Inn is close to many major businesses, shopping, dining, and leisure activities. Within walking distance are city and state government offices, the World Trade Center, the Convention Center, Farmers Market, and the Blue Line rapid transit.

Gracious hospitality awaits guests in the Brassers' home. These innkeepers have a reputation for friendliness and fabulous food. Enjoy coffee in the kitchen and a scrumptious breakfast in the dining room or outdoors in the fresh sea air on one of the porches. Treat yourself to a rarity these days: hand-ironed bed sheets. Learn more on the Web, www.lordmayors.com

Lord Mayor's Bed & Breakfast Inn
435 Cedar Avenue
Long Beach, CA 90802
562-436-0324
Fax 562-436-0324

Apple Pecan Bread

Dust this rich, moist bread with powdered sugar for a great breakfast bread. "This is a wonderful way to meet the needs of those with milk allergies," said Innkeeper Laura Brasser. She also serves it for dessert, topped with vanilla sauce. Makes 2 loaves.

    2 cups flour
    2 cups sugar (less if apples are sweet)
    2 teaspoons baking soda
    2 teaspoons mace
    ½ teaspoon salt
    2 cups raisins
    2 cups chopped pecans
    ½ cup vegetable oil
    2 eggs, beaten
    3 cups unpeeled and chopped apples

■ Preheat oven to 350 degrees. Grease 2 9 x 5-inch or 8 x 4-inch loaf pans.

■ In a large bowl, mix together the flour, sugar, baking soda, mace, and salt. Stir in the raisins and pecans.

■ Make a well in center of mixture. Pour in the oil, eggs, and apples; mix well

■ Spoon batter into loaf pans and bake for 1 hour, or until toothpick inserted in middle comes out clean.

White Mountain Lodge

C harlie and Mary Bast welcome guests to White Mountain Lodge with true Southwestern hospitality. The Lodge, considered the oldest building still standing in the Greer Basin, was built in 1892 as a family home. The two-story log house, constructed of timbers from the area, served mainly as the summer residence of the William Lund family, one of the first Mormon families to settle in Greer.

In 1904, the house was passed on to Lund's son, Marion, upon his marriage. Marion and Agnes, his spouse, converted the home into a year 'round residence, farming, raising eight children and adding onto the house as needed. When Marion retired from farming in 1940, the property was sold and transformed into the White Mountain Lodge by the new owners. Mary and Charlie left administrative positions in Tucson and bought the lodge and began renovation and remodeling in 1993. Each of the seven guestrooms is decorated in a Southwestern country style. The common rooms reflect the home's Southwest country heritage with period antiques, Southwest art and mission style furniture. A rock fireplace is a central feature of the living room. Also available for visitors are full housekeeping cabins, overlooking a gorgeous meadow and the Little Colorado River. Nestled in a remote mountain valley, Greer rarely sees summer temperatures above 76 degrees. The Greer Recreation Area offers opportunities for just about any outdoor activity, from hiking and fishing to down-hill and cross-country skiing. And those seeking to do more than just savor a mountain retreat love the Lodge's Murder Mystery Weekends. The Basts offer an exceptional made-from-scratch breakfast each morning. In the evening guests are treated to refreshments and homemade treats, and the cookie jar at White Mountain Lodge is always full. Learn more on the Web, www.wmonline.com/wmlodge

White Mountain Lodge

P.O. Box 143
140 Main Street
Greer, AZ 85927
520-735-7568 ■ Fax 520-735-7498

Apple Walnut Bread

"I started making this bread when a friend gave me a case of apples. It was not hard to get my children to help me peel, core, and slice the apples once they tasted the finished product!" recalled Innkeeper Mary Bast. "Now the kids are grown, and I use an apple peeler." Makes 2 loaves.

   1 cup sugar
  ½ cup butter-flavored shortening
  2 eggs
  1 teaspoon vanilla extract
  2 cups flour
  2 teaspoons cinnamon
  1 teaspoon nutmeg
  1 teaspoon baking powder
  1 teaspoon baking soda
  ½ teaspoon salt
  ½ teaspoon ground cloves
  4 medium-sized apples, chopped (about 2 cups)
  ½ cup chopped walnuts

- Preheat oven to 350 degrees. Grease and flour 2 9 x 5-inch loaf pans.
- With an electric mixer, beat together the sugar, shortening, eggs and vanilla until smooth.
- In a separate bowl, combine the flour, cinnamon, nutmeg, baking powder, baking soda, salt, and cloves.
- Stir the flour mixture and chopped apples into the sugar mixture by hand. Mix well. Fold in the walnuts.
- Pour batter into pans. Bake for 45 to 50 minutes, or until the center springs back when touched.

Angel Arbor
Bed & Breakfast Inn

*V*eteran Houston Innkeeper Marguerite Swanson, with her husband, Dean, opened Angel Arbor Bed & Breakfast Inn in September 1995 after a busy six-month restoration. Marguerite successfully operated Durham House B&B Inn, just a half-block away, for ten years before "downsizing" to this slightly smaller Georgian-style home. Both homes were once owned by Jay L. Durham, a Houston Heights benefactor. As father of eight, he aspired to acquire a house for each of his children, but he fell short of that goal because of the Great Depression.

Marguerite, a San Antonio native, easily moved into innkeeping as a profession. "I came from a big family and I was used to entertaining, and I just loved the idea of having people in my house all the time," she said. "I never have a day when I wake up and wish I were doing something else." Durham House quickly established a reputation for gracious accommodations and special occasions, such as unique murder mystery dinners, teas, showers, and small private parties.

In order to have more free time, she and Dean bought the elegant red brick residence that is now the Angel Arbor. It has five spacious guestrooms upstairs, three of which have double whirlpool tubs. The 1923 home, built for Katherine and John McTighe, had most recently been used for offices. The Swansons removed glued-down carpet, refinished the original hardwood floors, installed new bathrooms, and replaced many fixtures. They turned the screened porch into a year-round solarium overlooking the garden, with Marguerite's favorite angel statue and Dean's favorite vine-covered arbor. Guests enjoy the garden as well as the first-floor parlor, solarium, sunroom, and dining room. Learn more on the Web, www.angelarbor.com

Angel Arbor Bed & Breakfast Inn

848 Heights Boulevard
Houston, TX 77007
713-868-4654 ■ Toll-free 800-722-8788
Fax 713-861-3189

Applesauce Raisin Oatmeal Bread

"This is an easy-to-prepare bread that stores well. I frequently serve it with whipped cream cheese as a spread," explains Innkeeper Marguerite Swanson. Makes 1 loaf.

    1 cup oats, old-fashioned rolled or quick-cooking
1⅔ cups flour
    1 teaspoon cinnamon
    1 teaspoon baking soda
    ¼ teaspoon baking powder
    ½ teaspoon salt
    ½ cup chopped walnuts
    ½ cup golden raisins
    ½ cup margarine, softened
    ¾ cup sugar
    2 eggs
    1 cup applesauce

Topping

    1 teaspoon sugar
    ¼ teaspoon cinnamon

- Preheat oven to 350 degrees. Grease a 9 x 5-inch loaf pan.
- In a large bowl, combine the oats, flour, cinnamon, baking soda, baking powder, and salt. Stir in the walnuts and raisins.
- With an electric mixer, cream the margarine and sugar until light and fluffy. Add the eggs, and beat well.
- Add the dry ingredients and the applesauce alternately to the sugar mix, beating until smooth after each addition.
- Pour batter into pan.
- In a small bowl, mix sugar and cinnamon. Sprinkle the topping over the batter.
- Bake for 45 minutes, or until a toothpick inserted in the middle comes out clean.
- Cool on a rack for 10 minutes before removing from pan.

The Graham Bed & Breakfast Inn and Adobe Village

*S*edona, set among the beautiful red rocks that have become popular with travelers everywhere, was discovered by Carol and Roger Redenbaugh in 1992. When they stumbled upon The Graham Inn there, they knew they were "home." Having never stayed in a B&B, they instinctively knew that they wanted to be innkeepers. They wrote a business plan on the airplane back to Virginia, found it worked, and flew back the next weekend to finalize the sale. That caused their friends to say, "You're doing WHAT? WHERE?"

The Inn, first in Arizona to be built as a B&B, has six guestrooms, each with private balconies with red rock views, whirlpool tubs and fireplaces and other amenities. In 1997, the Redenbaughs added Adobe Village next door to the main inn, with four luxurious Santa Fe adobe-style cottages centered around a landscaped courtyard. Features include waterfall showers, bath fireplaces, one-of-a-kind furnishings and bread makers. Each casita is of totally different southwest architectural design and decor.

All of the guests enjoy the outdoor pool, hot tub, bicycles, and CD and video collection. Carol and Roger's guests gather before dinner for hors d'oeuvres and conversation, and can sneak homemade cookies from the cookie jar before bed.

The Redenbaughs provide an area map and make suggestions for everything from hiking to vortexes in the red rocks to art galleries and restaurants. Horseback riding, jeep tours, exploring Indian ruins, visiting Slide Rock State Park and shopping are among the favorite activities of guests. Learn more on the Web, www.sedonasfinest.com

The Graham Bed & Breakfast Inn and Adobe Village

150 Canyon Circle Drive
Sedona, AZ 86351
Toll-free 800-228-1425
Fax 520-284-0767

Apricot Banana Bread

At the Graham B&B Inn and Adobe Village, this bread is a perennial favorite served toasted, when the apricot bits get warm and chewy. This is just part of hearty breakfasts that have earned Innkeepers Carol and Roger Redenbaugh raves for years. Makes 1 regular loaf or 3 mini loaves.

   2 cups flour
   1 teaspoon baking powder
  ½ teaspoon baking soda
  ½ teaspoon salt
   1 cup sugar
  ½ cup dried apricots, chopped
  ½ cup chopped walnuts or shelled pistachios
  ¾ cup mashed ripe banana
  ½ cup milk
   1 egg
  ¼ cup melted butter or margarine
      whipped honey butter

■ Preheat oven to 350 degrees. Grease a 9 x 5-inch loaf pan or 3 small 3 x 5½ inch loaf pans.
■ In a large bowl, stir together flour, baking powder, baking soda, salt and sugar.
■ Stir in chopped apricots and nuts, mixing until nuts and apricots are well-coated.
■ In a separate bowl, combine banana, milk, egg and butter.
■ Stir banana mixture into dry ingredients just until all are well-blended.
■ Turn batter into pan or pans. Bake for about 45 minutes for mini-loaves, 50 to 60 minutes for large loaf, or until bread begins to shrink from the side of the pans.
■ Let bread cool in pans for 10 minutes, then turn out to rack to cool. Serve slices toasted with whipped honey butter.

Island Escape Bed & Breakfast

*G*uests at Island Escape revel in privacy — this B&B contains a single suite. The spacious accommodations include a living room finished in Hawaiian decor and a whirlpool bath. This contemporary home overlooks Puget Sound and the Olympic Mountains; a spectacular view of Mount Rainier awaits at the Fox Island bridge, just a short hike away.

Activities in this area of the Pacific Northwest run the gamut from action (scuba diving, windsurfing, sailing, mountain climbing) to total relaxation (beach-combing, bird- and wildlife-watching, reading). Nearby, the quaint fishing village of Gig Harbor hosts a myriad of events throughout the year, including parades, salmon bakes, local theatre productions, Autumn Apple Squeezing, and a summer art festival.

By concentrating on one set of guests at a time, innkeeper Paula Pascoe has found a variety of ways to pamper her visitors. Breakfast is served in the privacy of the suite; Paula features tasty, low-fat cuisine including such specialties as crab, ham, or veggie quiche, homemade granola, whole wheat huckleberry pancakes, and warm quick bread with French butter. She often strolls out to pluck fresh mint sprigs and edible flowers in season to complement the breakfast trays. E-mail address is paula@island-escape.com

Island Escape Bed & Breakfast
210 Island Blvd.
Fox Island, WA 98333
253-549-2044

Apricot Bread

This is a delicious quick bread to accompany breakfast or to serve to family and friends as an afternoon snack. "Use of dried apricots means you can always have some on hand in the pantry and the season won't make any difference," said Paula Pascoe, innkeeper, who got the recipe from a college friend. Makes 1 loaf.

> 1 cup dried apricots, chopped
> warm water
> 2 cups flour
> 2 teaspoons baking powder
> $\frac{1}{4}$ teaspoon baking soda
> $\frac{1}{2}$ teaspoon salt
> 1 cup sugar
> 2 tablespoons butter
> 1 egg
> 1 cup milk
> $\frac{1}{2}$ cup chopped nuts
> plain bread crumbs

- Cover the dried apricots with warm water. Cover and soak the apricots for at least 30 minutes or overnight.
- Grease a 9 x 5-inch loaf pan and sprinkle with plain bread crumbs.
- Drain the apricots and cut them with clean kitchen scissors into $\frac{1}{4}$-inch pieces.
- In a large bowl, sift together the flour, baking powder, baking soda, and salt.
- With an electric mixer, beat together the sugar, butter, and egg.
- Beat the dry ingredients into the sugar mixture alternately with the milk. Stir in the $\frac{1}{2}$ cup chopped nuts and the chopped apricots by hand.
- Pour batter into pan. Let stand for 20 minutes while preheating the oven to 350 degrees.
- Bake for 45 to 50 minutes, or until a toothpick inserted in the middle comes out clean. Let cool before slicing.

Angel Arbor
Bed & Breakfast Inn

*V*eteran Houston Innkeeper Marguerite Swanson, with her husband, Dean, opened Angel Arbor Bed & Breakfast Inn in September 1995 after a busy six-month restoration. Marguerite successfully operated Durham House B&B Inn, just a half-block away, for ten years before "downsizing" to this slightly smaller Georgian-style home. Both homes were once owned by Jay L. Durham, a Houston Heights benefactor. As father of eight, he aspired to acquire a house for each of his children, but he fell short of that goal because of the Great Depression.

Marguerite, a San Antonio native, easily moved into innkeeping as a profession. "I came from a big family and I was used to entertaining, and I just loved the idea of having people in my house all the time," she said. "I never have a day when I wake up and wish I were doing something else." Durham House quickly established a reputation for gracious accommodations and special occasions, such as unique murder mystery dinners, teas, showers, and small private parties.

In order to have more free time, she and Dean bought the elegant red brick residence that is now the Angel Arbor. It has five spacious guestrooms upstairs, three of which have double whirlpool tubs. The 1923 home, built for Katherine and John McTighe, had most recently been used for offices. The Swansons removed glued-down carpet, refinished the original hardwood floors, installed new bathrooms, and replaced many fixtures. They turned the screened porch into a year-round solarium overlooking the garden, with Marguerite's favorite angel statue and Dean's favorite vine-covered arbor. Guests enjoy the garden as well as the first-floor parlor, solarium, sunroom, and dining room. Learn more on the Web, www.angelarbor.com

Angel Arbor Bed & Breakfast Inn
848 Heights Boulevard
Houston, TX 77007
713-868-4654 ■ Toll-free 800-722-8788
Fax 713-861-3189

Apricot Orange Pecan Bread

"The flavor of this bread improves if it is tightly wrapped and stored in the refrigerator,"
said Marguerite Swanson, innkeeper. Makes 2 small loaves.

1 $\frac{1}{4}$ cups dried apricots, cut with kitchen shears
1 cup boiling water
1 cup sugar
3 tablespoons butter
2 $\frac{1}{2}$ cups flour
1 $\frac{1}{2}$ teaspoons baking soda
$\frac{1}{2}$ teaspoon salt
1 cup chopped pecans
2 eggs, beaten
$\frac{1}{2}$ cup orange juice

- Preheat oven to 350 degrees. Grease and flour 2 3 x 7-inch loaf pans.
- Place chopped apricots in a large bowl and add the boiling water, sugar and butter. Stir until the butter has melted and the sugar has dissolved. Cool.
- In a separate bowl, stir together the flour, baking soda, and salt. Stir into the cooled apricot mixture.
- Stir in pecans, eggs and orange juice until the mixture is evenly combined but still slightly lumpy.
- Bake for 60 minutes or until a toothpick inserted in the center comes out clean.
- Remove pans from oven, let sit for a few minutes, then invert. Cool on a rack. Wrap in plastic wrap and refrigerate until serving.

The Blue Spruce Inn

*S*ince 1989 The Blue Spruce Inn, once a simple village farm, has been Soquel's only B&B. Visitors enjoy the inn's six unique guestrooms plus in-room spas, comfortable lounge furniture, a shady grape arbor, and a "musical" pond — all on the north crest of beautiful Monterey Bay.

Innkeepers Pat and Tom O'Brien consider breakfast "an event." Guests arrive at the parlor to find steaming cups of coffee waiting. Good food and good company guarantee ample fuel for the day's events, which might include hiking among redwoods, cycling along the beach, tasting delicious locally vinted wines, searching for treasures at inviting antique shops, or watching whales and elephant seals along the coast. Monterey and Carmel are great day trips; in the evening, fine gourmet dining is within walking distance. At nightfall, contented visitors snuggle on premier feather beds, with pillows fluffed for dreams about the next day's activities. E-mail address is innkeeper@BlueSpruce.com

The Blue Spruce Inn
2815 South Main Street
Soquel, CA 95073
831-464-1137
Fax 831-475-0608
Toll free 800-559-1137

Aunt Nadine's Buttermilk Nut Bread

"This is one of several great 'Aunt Nadine' recipes I have saved over many years," explains Innkeeper Pat O'Brien. "Aunt Nadine was the great hostess of our family, always providing a complete celebration with such apparent ease when our families got together. This bread was always one of the special treats that went along with stories about life on the farm, growing up in the country, and working on the railroad." She adds that this bread slices better when baked the day before, and it freezes beautifully. Makes 1 loaf.

> 1 egg
> 1 cup brown sugar, packed
> 2 tablespoons shortening, melted
> 2 cups flour
> ¾ teaspoon baking powder
> ½ teaspoon baking soda
> ½ teaspoon salt
> 1 cup buttermilk
> 1 cup chopped nuts, divided

- Preheat oven to 350 degrees. Grease and flour a 9 x 5-inch loaf pan
- In a large mixing bowl, beat the egg well, then add the brown sugar and shortening.
- In a separate bowl, sift together the flour, baking powder, baking soda, and salt.
- Add the flour mixture alternately with the buttermilk to the egg mixture. Fold in ¾ cup of the nuts.
- Pour batter into pan. Sprinkle the top of the batter with the remaining ¼ cup of the nuts and gently press into the batter.
- Bake for 1 hour, or until a toothpick inserted in the middle comes out clean. Cool completely on a wire rack.

Martin Oaks Bed & Breakfast

*I*n 1990, Marie Vogl Gery and husband Frank bought this home, listed on the National Register of Historic Places and located on the Cannon River. The first portion of Sara Etta Archibald Martin's home was built in 1855, just a few years after her brothers and cousin founded the town of Dundas; the "addition," where the three guestrooms are located, was constructed in 1869. Rooms are designed to take guests back into the romance and elegance of the past. High beds have down pillows and comforters. And there's always a bedtime treat: brownies, brandy snaps, or fresh fruit.

Guests of Martin Oaks dine on fine china by candlelight, and breakfast always includes homebaked breads or muffins, an entrée, and dessert. Enjoy blueberry muffins with blueberry filling, lemon yogurt Bundt cakes, fresh basil omelettes, spicy pepper eggs or Martin Oaks Signature French Toast with meringue topping.

Marie and Frank encourage guests to take the historic walking tour through this town of 422, or relax on the veranda or in the parlor. Some choose to read *The Mystery of the House with Four Stairs,* a delightful story about this house written half a century ago. Marie, a professional storyteller, can fill visitors in on both past and present.

Martin Oaks B&B

107 First Street
P.O. Box 207
Dundas, MN 55019
507-645-4644

Banana Pecan Bread

"Living in Mississippi during WWII introduced our Iowa family to new tastes," recalls Innkeeper Marie Gery. "Mother got this recipe from Mrs. Celessie, who always wore white gloves and a hat whenever she left her house — if only to check her goldfish in the yard. Be sure to add the topping. The smell of cinnamon is part of a lovely memory." Makes 1 loaf.

    ½ cup butter, softened
    1 cup sugar
    3 large ripe bananas, mashed (keep separate)
    2 eggs
    1 teaspoon baking soda
pinch salt
    2 cups flour
    1 cup chopped pecans

Topping
    1 tablespoon butter, melted
    1 teaspoon cinnamon
    1 tablespoon sugar

- Preheat oven to 350 degrees. Spray a 9 x 5-inch loaf pan with non-stick cooking spray, then "sugar" it (sugar the pan just as you would flour it, coating the inside with sugar and then shaking out the excess).
- With an electric mixer, cream the butter and sugar. Beat in the bananas, one at a time. Beat in the eggs, also one at a time.
- In a separate bowl, mix the baking soda, salt, and flour.
- Add the flour mixture to the banana mixture ⅓ at a time and mix after each addition. Stir in the nuts.
- Turn the batter into pan. Bake for 50 to 60 minutes or until a toothpick inserted in the center comes out clean.
- While bread is baking, combine the melted butter, cinnamon, and sugar. When the bread is done baking, sprinkle the topping over the warm bread.

The Bagley House

*T*his 1772 country home is owned and operated by "the two Sues," as friends and colleagues know them: Susan Backhouse and Suzanne O'Connor. Former nurses "in another lifetime," the Sues chose this country location for their inn, just a ten-minute drive from downtown Freeport, with its famous L.L. Bean headquarters store and outlet shopping. They enjoy the peace and quiet of the country but also appreciate the proximity to stores, restaurants, museums, and colleges.

The Bagley House is a Greek Revival- and Colonial-style farmhouse, now situated on six acres (which include blueberry bushes, from which many a morning meal has been made!). Furnished with antiques and featuring the original wide "pumpkin pine" floors in many rooms, the home has one guestroom downstairs and four upstairs. Originally it was built as an inn, and now, after many years of other uses, it has come full circle. In 1998, the Sues added a modified Post-and-Beam style barn just a stone's throw from the main house, with three guestrooms. The Bliss Barn, as it is known, is very private and quiet and has views of the field and woods. The Androscoggin Room has a woodburning stove where guests can curl up to read or talk or to use as a conference room.

In the main house, guests can enjoy the library or gather in the kitchen around the brick fireplace and large table, chatting while breakfast is being prepared. Susan Backhouse, originally from England, often prepares authentic scones, English muffins, or other fare from old family recipes, and she willingly explains the differences from Americanized versions. Both Sues are well-versed on area activities and dining and are happy to help their guests explore the area. Learn more on the Web, http://members.aol.com/bedandbreak/bagley

The Bagley House
1290 Royalsborough Road
Durham, ME 04222
207-865-6566 ■ Fax 207-353-5878

Banana Walnut Bread

This is a very dense and moist bread, not overly sweet. Serve in thick wedges with whipped butter or cream cheese. "It also freezes very well," said Innkeeper Susan Backhouse. Makes 1 Bundt pan or 2 bread loaves.

$2\frac{1}{2}$ cups flour (2 cups white and $\frac{1}{2}$ cup whole-wheat if desired)

1 cup sugar

$1\frac{1}{4}$ teaspoons baking soda

$1\frac{1}{4}$ teaspoons baking powder

1 teaspoon salt

1 heaping tablespoon powdered buttermilk

$\frac{2}{3}$ cup vegetable oil

$\frac{1}{3}$ cup water

3 large, ripe bananas, cut into chunks

1 teaspoon vanilla extract

$\frac{1}{3}$ cup milk

2 eggs

$\frac{1}{2}$ cup chopped walnuts

- Preheat oven to 350 degrees. Grease a Bundt pan or 2 $8\frac{1}{4}$ x $4\frac{1}{4}$-inch loaf pans.
- Sift into a mixing bowl the flour, sugar, baking soda, baking powder, salt, and powdered buttermilk.
- Add oil, water, bananas, and vanilla extract. Beat with electric mixer at regular speed for 2 minutes.
- Add milk and eggs. Beat for 2 more minutes. Fold in walnuts.
- Bake for 1 hour (or about 50 minutes if 2 loaf pans are used) or until a toothpick inserted in the center comes out clean. "Do not open the oven during baking for at least 45 minutes," warns a Sue. Turn oven off and leave in the oven for 10 minutes.

The Doanleigh Inn

*T*he Doanleigh Inn, Kansas City's first B&B, was named after one of the original innkeeper's great-great-great grandmothers, Sarah Doanleigh of Wales. The current innkeepers, Cynthia Brogdon and Terry Maturo, purchased the grand inn in 1985 and have begun extensive renovations of the 1907 Georgian mansion, once a majestic private home.

The couple's interest in innkeeping began after Cynthia spent several years traveling throughout the country on business. Tiring of hotels and seeking more personalized service in a relaxed atmosphere, she began staying in B&Bs and country inns. Today, as innkeepers, Cynthia and Terry try to offer the service and pampering for their business and leisure guests that they would appreciate themselves. Computer modem access in guestrooms, early breakfasts, in-room speaker phones, and other conveniences are all efforts to meet the needs of business travelers. And, while the breakfast may be served as early as 6:00 in the morning, it is still delicious gourmet fare that has earned Cynthia quite a reputation. Guests enjoy evening hors d'oeuvres and wine, as well.

In the heart of Kansas City, the Doanleigh Inn overlooks historic Hyde Park, just 12 minutes from downtown. It is closer still to the famed Country Club Plaza, Hallmark Crown Center, and the University of Missouri, and it is near the Nelson-Atkins Museum of Art and other attractions. Learn more on the Web, www.doanleigh.com

The Doanleigh Inn
217 East 37th Street
Kansas City, MO 64111
816-753-2667
Fax 816-531-5185

Banana White Chocolate Loaf

"I made this loaf quite by accident one day, but it has turned out to be a house favorite," *says Innkeeper Cynthia Brogdon. She had to make substitutions in a recipe when she* *found herself out of some of the ingredients, and now is glad it happened. Makes 2 loaves.*

    3½ cups flour
     4 teaspoons baking powder
     1 teaspoon baking soda
     1 teaspoon cinnamon
     1 teaspoon nutmeg
     1 teaspoon salt
     2 cups ripe bananas, mashed
    1½ cups sugar
     2 eggs
     ½ cup butter, melted
     ½ cup evaporated milk
     2 cups chopped nuts
     1 12-ounce package white chocolate chips

- Preheat oven to 350 degrees. Grease and flour 2 9 x 5-inch loaf pans.
- In a large bowl, stir together the flour, baking powder, baking soda, cinnamon, nutmeg, and salt.
- In a separate bowl, beat the bananas, sugar, eggs, and butter until creamy.
- Add the dry ingredients alternately with the milk to the banana mixture, mixing until well blended.
- Stir in the nuts and chips.
- Pour batter into pans. Bake for 1 hour, or until a toothpick inserted in the middle comes out clean.

Inn on the Rio

*L*ocated on the Rio Fernando at the base of the Sangre de Cristo Mountains, just east from historic downtown Taos Plaza, the Inn on the Rio has recently been re-born. Innkeepers Robert and Julie Chahalane left the corporate "rat race" back in New England and took on the monumental task of bringing a former landmark back into its glory. Julie, with a master's degree in nutrition, knew she could satisfy her guests' hunger for healthy Southwest treats. Robert, a retired marketing executive with an background in finance and economics, knew he could make the numbers work. But what about the declining physical structures? New friends and neighbors, happy to see the interest of the new innkeepers, offered their knowledge, and the task began.

One renovation highlight is an outdoor, in-ground hot tub that offers a spectacular view of Taos Mountain during the day and the star-studded sky at night. Rooms are decorated in "cowboy casual" and "pueblo picturesque" with blankets, rugs, and art collected from all over New Mexico. Julie's new flowerbeds are filled with hollyhocks, Mexican Hats, and other native plants. The "icing on the cake" has been visits by two Southwest artists who spent several weeks painting murals on the exterior walls, arches over the doorways, and, with painstaking detail, the interiors, including each bathroom! In front of the historic Carmen Valarde Kiva fireplace in the inn's cozy gathering room, Julie offers guests suggestions for dining, sightseeing, and shopping. Robert, an outdoor enthusiast, reveals the best-kept secrets of the great outdoors for close-by hiking, mountain biking, and challenging skiing. Learn more on the Web, www.innontherio.com

Inn on the Rio

Box 6529-NDCBU
910 East Kit Carson Road
Taos, NM 87571
505-758-7199 ■ Fax 505-751-1816
Toll-free 800-859-6752

Breakfast Pear Loaf

"A wonderful alternative to banana bread, Breakfast Pear Loaf is moist and delicious. It has become a requested favorite among the guests," notes Innkeeper Julie Cahalane. "This recipe can easily be doubled." Makes 1 loaf.

$\frac{1}{2}$ cup butter, softened
1 cup sugar
2 eggs
$\frac{1}{4}$ cup milk
1 teaspoon vanilla extract
2 cups flour
1 teaspoon baking powder
$\frac{1}{2}$ teaspoon baking soda
$\frac{1}{4}$ teaspoon nutmeg
1 cup coarsely chopped pears
$\frac{1}{2}$ cup chopped walnuts or pecans

■ Preheat oven to 350 degrees. Grease a 9 x 5-inch glass loaf pan.
■ With an electric mixer, beat together the butter and sugar until creamy. Add the eggs, milk, vanilla, and mix well.
■ In a separate bowl, sift together the flour, baking powder, baking soda and nutmeg. Combine the dry ingredients with the butter mixture and stir thoroughly.
■ Fold in the chopped pears and nuts. Stir until just blended.
■ Pour batter into pan. Bake for 1 hour, or until a toothpick inserted in the middle comes out clean.

Window on the Winds

*L*eanne McClain's two-story log home is the perfect base for a Wyoming vacation. The second floor, with four guestrooms featuring lodgepole pine beds, is reserved for guests. A view of the Wind River Mountains from the fireside gathering room has been known to take more than one guest's breath away.

Leanne is an archeologist who enjoys sharing her perspective on the area and can offer information about the history of the Green River Basin and the Wind River Range. She is also happy to help guests plan their fishing, rafting, riding, skiing, or hiking adventures.

Window on the Winds is located directly on the Continental Divide Snowmobile Trail at elevation 7,175 feet. A guided inn-to-inn snowmobile tour that leads into Yellowstone National Park leaves right from the property. Guests can snowmobile from the front door, through the Wind River Mountains and on into Yellowstone National Park. Other winter adventures include dog sledding and racing, and both cross-country and downhill skiing.

Whatever the season, guests can return from a day of outdoor adventure to relax and enjoy the hot tub. Fresh fruits, vegetables, and whole grains are always on the breakfast menu. Leanne specializes in western hospitality, even offering to board guests' horses. The bed and breakfast is within a two-hour drive of Jackson Hole and the Grand Teton and Yellowstone National Parks. Learn more on the Web, www.cruising-america.com/windowonwinds

Window on the Winds Bed & Breakfast
10151 Highway 191, P.O. Box 996
Pinedale, WY 82941
307-367-2600
Fax 307-367-2395
Toll-free 888-367-1345

Bronco Beer Bread

"This bread is named Bronco Beer Bread because it is my Grandma's recipe," said Inn-keeper Leanne McClain. "She was a Denver Broncos football fan. Her original recipe instructed you to put the bread in a moderate oven at kick-off time, and that it would be done at half-time." Makes 1 loaf.

> 3 **cups self-rising flour, unsifted**
> 2 **tablespoons sugar**
> 1 **can (12 ounces) beer, room temperature**

- Preheat oven to 375 degrees. Liberally grease a 9 x 5-inch loaf pan.
- Place the flour, sugar, and beer in a bowl. Stir 17 times, until the dry ingredients are moist.
- Turn the dough into pan, spreading it fairly evenly (dough will be sticky).
- Bake for approximately 1 hour or until bread is brown and pulls away from the sides of the pan.

Yankee Hill Inn Bed & Breakfast

*T*he ambiance of quiet, small town life in the heart of the Kettle Moraine recreational area is what Yankee Hill Inn Bed and Breakfast Innkeepers Peg and Jim Stahlman find draws guests to their two historic homes-turned-B&Bs.

Yankee Hill Inn B&B is comprised of two historic homes restored by the Stahlmans. One is a Sheboygan County landmark, a Queen Anne Victorian–style, built in 1891. The other is an 1870 Gothic Italianate listed on the National Register of Historic Places. Both were built in the "Yankee Hill" area of Plymouth by hard-working, affluent brothers, Henry and Gilbert Huson.

Yankee Hill Inn has 12 guestrooms, decorated with period antiques and other touches to reflect historic lodging. Six guestrooms have single whirlpool tubs. Landscaped yards, parlors, fireplaces, and an enclosed front porch allow the guests to gather and relax. Each morning, guests wake up to the aroma of a full breakfast, featuring home-baked muffins and breads, and the cookie jar is open to guests.

From the Inn, guests take a short walk through Huson Park and across the Mullet River footbridge into downtown Plymouth, where they can explore charming antique and gift shops and dine in excellent restaurants. At the Plymouth Center is an art gallery, the Plymouth Historical Museum, and visitor information.

Outdoor adventures surround Plymouth in the glacially sculpted terrain. Enjoy the Kettle Moraine State Forest, many lakes, marked nature trails and the Ice Age Trail for hiking and biking. The paved Old Plank Road recreational trail, historic Plymouth walking tour, Road America race track and the Kohler Design Center, featuring the latest in Kohler bathroom and kitchen ideas, are also popular. Sheboygan and Lake Michigan are just 15 minutes away. Learn more on the Web, www.yankeehillinn.com

Yankee Hill Inn Bed & Breakfast
405 Collins Street
Plymouth, WI 53073
920-892-2222 ■ Fax 920-892-6228

Butter Swirl Loaf

"Isn't it wonderful how innkeepers' friends like to share their recipes for use at the Inn? This one comes from my friend, Nancy, who's a great cook," noted Peg Stahlman. "It uses basic ingredients found in every kitchen, and it smells heavenly while baking." Makes 1 loaf.

  2 eggs
½ cup sugar
½ cup butter, melted
  2 cups flour
  3 teaspoons baking powder
½ teaspoon salt
¾ cup milk

Topping

⅓ cup sugar
  2 teaspoons cinnamon
¼ cup butter, melted

- Preheat oven to 375 degrees. Grease and flour a 9 x 5-inch loaf pan.
- With an electric mixer, beat the eggs until thick. Add the sugar and ¼ cup butter.
- In a separate bowl, stir together the flour, baking powder, and salt. Stir the dry ingredients into the egg mixture alternately with the milk, blending well.
- Pour batter into pan.
- To make the topping, combine the sugar and cinnamon. Sprinkle over the batter. Pour the remaining ¼ cup melted butter over the batter. Cut through the batter with a knife, swirling the topping.
- Bake for 40 to 45 minutes.

Watch Hill Bed & Breakfast

*W*hen guests come to Barbara Lauterbach's B&B, they may come for many reasons — but when they come *back*, "food" is always one that draws them. A gourmet chef, Barbara trained at renowned culinary institutes in Paris, Italy, and England. Her food-related career has included developing cooking schools for a chain of department stores, serving as an instructor at the New England Culinary Institute, and acting as a consultant and spokesperson for food-related businesses. She also has done regular television cooking segments and presents classes around the country. When she bought the B&B in 1989, her background was just one of the talents that made innkeeping attractive to her. Guests love to sit and chat during an excellent breakfast, and Barbara holds cooking classes at the B&B.

Watch Hill is one of the oldest homes in Center Harbor. Built circa 1772 by the brother of the town's founder, it has views of Lake Winnipesaukee, just down the street. Guests in the four guestrooms especially enjoy the home's porch in the summer or warming up with a mug of hot cider after skiing or snowmobiling in the winter. Barbara's full country breakfast often showcases New Hampshire products and may feature fresh, hot breads, sausage, bacon, home-fries, fresh fruit, and brown eggs. Guests enjoy the food and the conversation, which often turns to the how her B&B was named (after the champion bull mastiffs Barbara used to raise from the Watch Hill kennel in Cincinnati, Ohio). Watch Hill is a five-minute walk from one of the country's foremost quilt shops, and quilters are frequent guests. "Sometimes they come in vans and take over the whole place!" Barbara said. "They have Show and Tell in the evening, inspecting each other's purchases of fabrics and patterns."

Watch Hill Bed & Breakfast
P.O. Box 1605
Center Harbor, NH 03226
603-253-4334 ■ Fax 603-253-8560

Cheddar Sausage Bread

In this recipe, ham or crumbled bacon may be substituted for the sausage. Instead of the traditional loaf pan, try baking this bread in a lightly greased 9-inch round cake pan or iron skillet for 30 to 45 minutes. Serve warm with sweet butter. Makes 1 loaf.

- 1 cup flour
- 1 cup white whole-wheat flour (King Arthur blend preferred)
- 1 tablespoon baking powder
- ½ teaspoon baking soda
- ½ teaspoon salt
- 1 cup grated Cheddar cheese
- 1 tablespoon caraway or dill seed
- 1 cup diced hard sausage
- 1 cup chopped onion
- 2 eggs
- 1 cup sour cream, buttermilk, or yogurt
- 2 tablespoons butter, melted, or vegetable oil

- Preheat oven to 350 degrees. Grease a 9 x 5-inch loaf pan.
- In a large bowl, combine the flour, whole-wheat flour, baking powder, baking soda, and salt.
- Stir in the cheese, caraway or dill seed, sausage, and onion.
- In a separate bowl, beat the eggs. Add the sour cream to the eggs and beat well. Add the egg mixture to the flour mixture, mixing just enough to blend.
- Pour batter into pan. Bake for 50 to 60 minutes. Serve warm.

Whitefish Bay Farm
Bed & Breakfast

*T*his restored 1908 American Foursquare farmhouse has been open as a bed and breakfast since 1991. Innkeepers Dick and Gretchen Regnery run a working farm here as well, raising tranquil Corriedale sheep and famous Door County cherries.

The names of Whitefish Bay Farm's guestrooms evoke the delightful flowers that dot nearby meadows and orchards each spring: Buttercup Room; Trillium Room; Apple Blossom Room; Iris Room. After a peaceful night surrounded by a charming assortment of quilts, handwoven wool rugs and throws, and original art, guests are greeted each morning with an abundant from-scratch breakfast in the Scandinavian-style dining room.

A visit to the B&B's art gallery in the granary barn is a must; a unique collection of photos and fiber art is on display here from Memorial Day weekend until mid-October. Weaving and hand spinning take place daily, using wool from the Regnery's own sheep.

The farm is located next to the rolling sand beaches of Whitefish Dunes State Park, near the popular — but secluded — sites of Clark Lake and Cave Point. Guests also have easy access to Door County's scenic backroad bicycle routes. Learn more on the Web, www.whitefishbayfarm.com

Whitefish Bay Farm B&B
3831 Clark Lake Road (County WD)
Sturgeon Bay, WI 54235
920-743-1560

Cherry Raisin Poppyseed Loaf

"This recipe was first given to me by my sister-in-law, who is not a cook or baker," noted Innkeeper Gretchen Regnery. "It called for lemon and blueberries," but Gretchen modified is using Door County's famous tart cherries and raisins. Makes 1 large or 3 small loaves.

> 1 cup sugar
> ¼ cup butter or margarine
> 2 eggs
> 1 teaspoon orange peel
> 2 cups flour
> 2½ teaspoons baking powder
> ¼ teaspoon nutmeg
> 1 cup milk
> ½ cup golden raisins
> ½ cup dried cherries
> ⅓ cup poppyseeds

- Preheat oven to 350 degrees. Liberally grease a 9 x 5-inch loaf pan or 3 3¼ x 5½-inch loaf pans.
- With an electric mixer, cream the sugar and butter. Add the eggs, 1 at a time, beating well after each addition. Add the orange peel.
- In a separate bowl, sift together the flour, baking powder, and nutmeg. Add the dry ingredients alternately with the milk to the butter mixture until well blended.
- Stir in the raisins, dried cherries, and poppyseeds.
- Turn the batter into pan. Bake large pan for 1 hour, or small pans for 45 to 50 minutes, or until a toothpick inserted in the middle comes out clean.
- Cool in the pan for 10 minutes, and then turn out onto a wire rack to cool completely.

The Doanleigh Inn

*T*he Doanleigh Inn, Kansas City's first B&B, was named after one of the original innkeeper's great-great-great grandmothers, Sarah Doanleigh of Wales. The current innkeepers, Cynthia Brogdon and Terry Maturo, purchased the grand inn in 1985 and have begun extensive renovations of the 1907 Georgian mansion, once a majestic private home.

The couple's interest in innkeeping began after Cynthia spent several years traveling throughout the country on business. Tiring of hotels and seeking more personalized service in a relaxed atmosphere, she began staying in B&Bs and country inns. Today, as innkeepers, Cynthia and Terry try to offer the service and pampering for their business and leisure guests that they would appreciate themselves. Computer modem access in guestrooms, early breakfasts, in-room speaker phones, and other conveniences are all efforts to meet the needs of business travelers. And, while the breakfast may be served as early as 6:00 in the morning, it is still delicious gourmet fare that has earned Cynthia quite a reputation. Guests enjoy evening hors d'oeuvres and wine, as well.

In the heart of Kansas City, the Doanleigh Inn overlooks historic Hyde Park, just 12 minutes from downtown. It is closer still to the famed Country Club Plaza, Hallmark Crown Center, and the University of Missouri, and it is near the Nelson-Atkins Museum of Art and other attractions. Learn more on the Web, www.doanleigh.com

The Doanleigh Inn

217 East 37th Street
Kansas City, MO 64111
816-753-2667
Fax 816-531-5185

Chocolate Pepper Pound Cake

"This unique pound cake has a great flavor! The pepper adds a little bite, which is a nice contrast to the sweetness of the chips," said Innkeeper Cynthia Brogdon. Makes 1 large loaf.

    1 cup butter
    1 cup sugar
    4 eggs
    1 tablespoon lemon juice
    1 teaspoon vanilla extract
 $1\frac{1}{2}$ cups flour
    1 teaspoon nutmeg
    1 teaspoon baking powder
   $\frac{3}{4}$ teaspoon freshly ground black pepper
   $\frac{1}{2}$ teaspoon baking soda
   $\frac{1}{4}$ teaspoon salt
   $\frac{1}{4}$ cup semi-sweet chocolate chips

- Preheat oven to 325 degrees. Grease a 9 x 5-inch loaf pan.
- With an electric mixer, cream the butter and sugar until smooth. Beat in the eggs, lemon juice, and vanilla.
- In a separate bowl, combine the flour, nutmeg, baking powder, black pepper, baking soda, and salt.
- Pour the dry ingredients into the butter mixture, stirring well. Fold in the chocolate chips.
- Pour batter into pan. Bake for 50 minutes, or until a toothpick inserted in the middle comes out clean.

Yankee Hill Inn Bed & Breakfast

*T*he ambiance of quiet, small town life in the heart of the Kettle Moraine recreational area is what Yankee Hill Inn Bed and Breakfast Innkeepers Peg and Jim Stahlman find draws guests to their two historic homes-turned-B&Bs.

Yankee Hill Inn B&B is comprised of two historic homes restored by the Stahlmans. One is a Sheboygan County landmark, a Queen Anne Victorian–style, built in 1891. The other is an 1870 Gothic Italianate listed on the National Register of Historic Places. Both were built in the "Yankee Hill" area of Plymouth by hard-working, affluent brothers, Henry and Gilbert Huson.

Yankee Hill Inn has 12 guestrooms, decorated with period antiques and other touches to reflect historic lodging. Six guestrooms have single whirlpool tubs. Land-scaped yards, parlors, fireplaces, and an enclosed front porch allow the guests to gather and relax. Each morning, guests wake up to the aroma of a full breakfast, featuring home-baked muffins and breads, and the cookie jar is open to guests.

From the Inn, guests take a short walk through Huson Park and across the Mullet River footbridge into downtown Plymouth, where they can explore charming antique and gift shops and dine in excellent restaurants. At the Plymouth Center is an art gallery, the Plymouth Historical Museum, and visitor information.

Outdoor adventures surround Plymouth in the glacially sculpted terrain. Enjoy the Kettle Moraine State Forest, many lakes, marked nature trails and the Ice Age Trail for hiking and biking. The paved Old Plank Road recreational trail, historic Plymouth walking tour, Road America race track and the Kohler Design Center, featuring the latest in Kohler bathroom and kitchen ideas, are also popular. Sheboygan and Lake Michigan are just 15 minutes away. Learn more on the Web, www.yankeehillinn.com

Yankee Hill Inn Bed & Breakfast

405 Collins Street
Plymouth, WI 53073
920-892-2222 ■ Fax 920-892-6228

Chocolate Tea Bread

"This wonderfully moist bread, with both cocoa and chocolate chips, is truly a chocolate-lovers delight." Innkeeper Peg Stahlman usually quadruples the recipe to always have a couple of extra loaves in the freezer. Makes 1 loaf.

1½ cups flour
1⅓ cups sugar
⅓ cup cocoa
1 teaspoon baking soda
¾ teaspoon salt
¼ teaspoon baking powder
⅓ cup margarine or shortening
2 eggs
½ cup applesauce
⅓ cup water
⅓ cup semi-sweet chocolate chips
⅓ cup chopped nuts

■ Preheat oven to 350 degrees. Grease and flour a 9 x 5-inch loaf pan.
■ In a large bowl, combine the flour, sugar, cocoa, baking soda, salt, and baking powder.
■ In a separate bowl, mix together the margarine or shortening, eggs, applesauce, and water. Combine with the dry ingredients.
■ Stir in the chocolate chips and nuts
■ Pour batter into pan. Bake for 1 hour.
■ Cool for 5 minutes, and then turn out onto a wire rack.

Whitefish Bay Farm
Bed & Breakfast

This restored 1908 American Foursquare farmhouse has been open as a bed and breakfast since 1991. Innkeepers Dick and Gretchen Regnery run a working farm here as well, raising tranquil Corriedale sheep and famous Door County cherries.

The names of Whitefish Bay Farm's guestrooms evoke the delightful flowers that dot nearby meadows and orchards each spring: Buttercup Room; Trillium Room; Apple Blossom Room; Iris Room. After a peaceful night surrounded by a charming assortment of quilts, handwoven wool rugs and throws, and original art, guests are greeted each morning with an abundant from-scratch breakfast in the Scandinavian-style dining room.

A visit to the B&B's art gallery in the granary barn is a must; a unique collection of photos and fiber art is on display here from Memorial Day weekend until mid-October. Weaving and hand spinning take place daily, using wool from the Regnery's own sheep.

The farm is located next to the rolling sand beaches of Whitefish Dunes State Park, near the popular — but secluded — sites of Clark Lake and Cave Point. Guests also have easy access to Door County's scenic backroad bicycle routes. Learn more on the Web, www.whitefishbayfarm.com

Whitefish Bay Farm B&B
3831 Clark Lake Road (County WD)
Sturgeon Bay, WI 54235
920-743-1560

Citrus Juice Bread

"Citrus Juice Bread is especially good for breakfast when served with a seasoned egg dish," said Innkeeper Gretchen Regnery. "It is also good as part of an afternoon tea. It's sweet and moist and light, with a nice citrus tang." Makes 1 loaf.

$1\frac{1}{4}$ cups sugar
$\frac{1}{2}$ cup margarine
2 eggs
$1\frac{1}{2}$ cups flour
1 teaspoon baking powder
$\frac{1}{4}$ cup orange juice
$\frac{1}{4}$ cup milk
1 teaspoon lemon peel
1 teaspoon orange peel

Glaze

1 tablespoon lemon juice
1 tablespoon orange juice
$\frac{1}{3}$ cup sugar

■ Preheat oven to 325 degrees. Spray a 9 x 5-inch loaf pan or 3 $3\frac{1}{4}$ x $5\frac{1}{2}$-inch loaf pans with non-stick cooking spray.

■ With an electric mixer, cream the sugar and margarine. Add the eggs and beat well.

■ In a small bowl, sift together the flour and baking powder (do not skip this step, or the bread will not be as light as it should be!)

■ Combine the $\frac{1}{4}$ cup orange juice with the milk. Add the flour mixture alternately with the orange juice mixture to the creamed mixture. Beat until very smooth. Stir in the lemon and orange peels.

■ Spoon batter into loaf pan. Bake large pan for 50 to 60 minutes, or small pans for 45 to 50 minutes, checking after 40 minutes, or until a toothpick inserted in the middle comes out clean.

■ During last five minutes of baking, prepare the glaze. In a saucepan over low heat, combine the lemon juice, orange juice, and sugar. Stir and blend until sugar is melted and glaze appears clear.

■ Remove bread from oven and spoon glaze immediately over it, dividing glaze equally among the three loaves. Cool completely in pan before slicing.

Lamb's Inn Bed & Breakfast

*D*ick and Donna Messerschmidt returned to the Little Willow Valley near Richland Center, Wisconsin, after 32 years away. They bought Donna's parents 180-acre dairy farm and completely restored the house to appear as it did when Albert Misslich brought his bride home in the late 1800s, adding modern conveniences.

The large kitchen, with Donna's grandmother's round oak table, is the center of the Bed & Breakfast, with a formal dining room, living room and library open to guests, as well. Coffee is often enjoyed on the enclosed porch. A new cottage, built in 1990 for Dick and Donna to live in while renovating the farmhouse, has two guest suites.

Breakfast, served in the dining room, is Donna and Dick's favorite part of innkeeping, where the conversation flows, as does hot coffee, for sometimes as long as two hours. Entreés that often appear include blueberry pancakes with an orange sauce, Italian quiche, or stuffed French toast with an apricot sauce. Warm muffins or bread and fresh fruit are always served, as well. In the fall, fresh applesauce and granola might be on the menu.

Guests enjoy feeding the trout in the backyard spring, petting the cats, watching the goats or just going for a quiet walk in the country. In nearby Spring Green, Frank Lloyd Wright's Taliesen and the House on the Rock can be toured, or guests can attend Shakespeare under the stars at American Players Theater. Guests also enjoy visiting Amish farms, canoeing the Kickapoo River or biking the Sparta-Elroy bike trail. Learn more on the Web, www.lambs-inn.com

Lamb's Inn Bed & Breakfast
23761 Misslich Road
Richland Center, WI 53581
608-585-4301

Coconut Bread

"This bread is moist, so it keeps well and also freezes well," said Innkeeper Donna Messerschmidt. *"It is good served cold or toasted lightly. It's quick and easy to make — a big help to a busy innkeeper or guest. I like to keep some in the freezer for busy days."* Makes 3 loaves.

>   1 cup butter, softened
>   2 cups sugar
>   4 eggs
>   4 teaspoons coconut extract
>   1 16-ounce carton sour cream
>   2 cups coconut
>   4 cups flour
>   2 teaspoons baking soda
>   2 teaspoons baking powder

- ■ Preheat oven to 350 degrees. Grease and flour 3 9 x 5-inch loaf pans.
- ■ In a very large mixing bowl, cream the butter and sugar. Beat in the eggs, coconut extract, and sour cream. Stir in the coconut.
- ■ In a separate bowl, stir together the flour, baking soda, and baking powder. Add the flour mixture to the batter.
- ■ Pour batter into pans. Bake for 50 minutes, or until a toothpick inserted in the middle comes out clean.
- ■ Let cool in the pan for 10 minutes, and then remove from the pans to cool completely on a wire rack.

Chambered Nautilus

*I*n May 1996, longtime Seattle residents Joyce Schulte and Steven Poole changed careers and became the third owners to welcome guests to this gracious inn. Built in 1915 by University of Washington professor Dr. Herbert Gowen and his wife, Anne, this elegant 1915 Georgian Colonial home perches on a peaceful hill in Seattle's University district. In the mid 1980s, the home was turned into a B&B. Joyce and Steve are collectors of antique oak furniture and several new pieces have been added to the collection. Recent remodeling projects have dressed up the inn by refinishing hardwood floors, adding and updating bathrooms, and remodeling an attic room to include a fireplace.

Chambered Nautilus offers six large, airy guestrooms, each outfitted with antiques and down comforters. Fresh flowers, bottled water, soft robes, and teddy bears welcome guests to each room, several of which overlook the gardens and the stunning Cascade Mountains. Guests are welcome to relax by the fire in the living room, indulging in fresh-baked cookies on the sunporch or in the garden, or delving into the extensive library. Breakfast is served in the elegant dining room or on the sunporch. Steve prepares the sumptuous meal, which includes fresh fruit, juice, granola, baked treats, and such unique entrées as Northwest Breakfast Pie. Of course, there's always plenty of fresh-roasted Seattle coffee! Guests will find plenty to do in the area. Downtown, visit the Pike Place Market, the Seattle Aquarium, the Klondike Gold Rush National Historical Park, or ride the ferries or the monorail. Wineries, waterfalls, the Woodland Park Zoo, restaurants, and plenty of outdoor recreation is also found in the area. Nearby is the Burke-Gilman trail for bikers and walkers and Ravenna Park. Learn more on the Web, www.chamberednautilus.com

Chambered Nautilus
5005 22nd Avenue NE
Seattle, WA 98105
206-522-2536 ■ Fax 206-528-0898

Cranberry Orange Bread

To make this year 'round, simply buy fresh cranberries in season and freeze them, advises Innkeeper Joyce Schulte. "Traditionally a holiday treat, guests love to be surprised with warm cranberry bread on the breakfast table in the middle of the summer!" Makes 1 loaf.

  2 tablespoons butter or margarine
  1 egg
  1 cup sugar
  ¾ cup orange juice
  ¼ teaspoon orange extract
  2 cups flour
  1 teaspoon baking powder
  ½ teaspoon baking soda
  ½ teaspoon salt
  2 cups whole, fresh cranberries (or fresh frozen; thaw before using)
  ½ cup chopped walnuts

- Preheat oven to 350 degrees. Grease a 9 x 5-inch loaf pan.
- With an electric mixer, combine the butter, egg, and sugar; mix well.
- Add the orange juice, orange extract, flour, baking powder, baking soda, and salt; stir until just moistened.
- Fold in the cranberries and nuts.
- Bake for 60 to 70 minutes, or until toothpick inserted in middle comes out clean.

Watch Hill Bed & Breakfast

When guests come to Barbara Lauterbach's B&B, they may come for many reasons — but when they come *back*, "food" is always one that draws them. A gourmet chef, Barbara trained at renowned culinary institutes in Paris, Italy, and England. Her food-related career has included developing cooking schools for a chain of department stores, serving as an instructor at the New England Culinary Institute, and acting as a consultant and spokesperson for food-related businesses. She also has done regular television cooking segments and presents classes around the country. When she bought the B&B in 1989, her background was just one of the talents that made innkeeping attractive to her. Guests love to sit and chat during an excellent breakfast, and Barbara holds cooking classes at the B&B.

Watch Hill is one of the oldest homes in Center Harbor. Built circa 1772 by the brother of the town's founder, it has views of Lake Winnipesaukee, just down the street. Guests in the four guestrooms especially enjoy the home's porch in the summer or warming up with a mug of hot cider after skiing or snowmobiling in the winter. Barbara's full country breakfast often showcases New Hampshire products and may feature fresh, hot breads, sausage, bacon, home-fries, fresh fruit, and brown eggs. Guests enjoy the food and the conversation, which often turns to the how her B&B was named (after the champion bull mastiffs Barbara used to raise from the Watch Hill kennel in Cincinnati, Ohio). Watch Hill is a five-minute walk from one of the country's foremost quilt shops, and quilters are frequent guests. "Sometimes they come in vans and take over the whole place!" Barbara said. "They have Show and Tell in the evening, inspecting each other's purchases of fabrics and patterns."

Watch Hill Bed & Breakfast
P.O. Box 1605
Center Harbor, NH 03226
603-253-4334 ■ Fax 603-253-8560

Creamy Double Corn Bread

Barbara Lauterbach, innkeeper at Watch Hill Bed & Breakfast, said this rich corn bread is deliciously moist and equally suitable for lunch or supper. Creamy Double Corn Bread can take on a southwest flavor with the addition of 2 tablespoons minced green and red bell pepper, or 1 tablespoon minced jalapeño pepper. Makes 1 loaf.

½ cup flour
½ cup cornmeal
2 teaspoons baking powder
1 cup plain yogurt or sour cream
1 can (8-ounces) cream-style corn
2 eggs
¼ cup vegetable oil
1 teaspoon salt
½ teaspoon sugar

- Preheat oven to 400 degrees. Grease and preheat an 8-inch cake pan or oven-proof skillet.
- In a large bowl, combine the flour, cornmeal, baking powder, yogurt or sour cream, corn, eggs, oil, salt, and sugar.
- Pour the batter into the preheated pan. Bake for 30 minutes, or until the bread pulls away from the sides of the pan.
- Serve warm in the skillet, or cut into squares.

Inn at Cedar Crossing

*A*t the Inn at Cedar Crossing, Innkeeper Terry Smith's guests are treated to a hearty continental breakfast that includes a number of wonderful creations by the Inn's pastry chef.

This Historic Register mercantile building was erected in 1884, with shops at street level and merchant's quarters upstairs. In 1985, Terry, a banker who was active in local historic preservation, purchased the building to remake into an inn. After extensive restoration, the upstairs was transformed into an inviting inn, and, later, the street level became an acclaimed restaurant with Victorian-era decor.

Today the inn has nine guestrooms with period antiques, custom-crafted poster and canopied beds, and elegant decor. Many of the guestrooms have fireplaces graced with antique mantels, double whirlpool tubs, private porches, and televisions and VCRs hidden in armoires. All of the rooms feature plump down-filled comforters and decorator fabrics, wallpapers, and linens. The Gathering Room is a relaxing spot for guests to gather by the fireplace and enjoy locally pressed apple cider, popcorn, and those homemade cookies fresh from the Inn's baking kitchen.

This Inn's restaurant has been named as one of the Top 25 restaurants in the state by the *Milwaukee Journal-Sentinel*. Open daily for all three meals, the restaurant specializes in fresh ingredients, enticingly prepared entrées, and sinful desserts, and a casual pub serves liquid refreshments. The Inn's guests head out to enjoy Door County's hiking, biking, antiquing, shopping, golfing, or just poking along the back roads of this scenic peninsula bordered by Lake Michigan. Learn more on the Web, www.innatcedarcrossing.com

Inn at Cedar Crossing

336 Louisiana Street
Sturgeon Bay, WI 54235
920-743-4200
Fax 920-743-4422

Double Chocolate Zucchini Bread

"This quick bread is very chocolatey and moist," said innkeeper Terry Smith, whose restaurant may offer this late-summer bread as part of the decadent breakfast menu. Using grocery-store zucchini, you can enjoy it nearly all year 'round. Makes 2 loaves.

3 eggs
2 cups sugar
1 cup vegetable oil
1 teaspoon vanilla
2 ounces unsweetened baking chocolate, melted
2 cups zucchini, grated
2 cups flour
1 teaspoon baking soda
1 teaspoon salt
1 teaspoon cinnamon
1 cup walnuts, chopped
$\frac{1}{2}$ cup semi-sweet chocolate chips

- Preheat oven to 350 degrees.
- With an electric mixer, beat eggs until light. While still beating, gradually add sugar, oil, and vanilla. Stir in melted chocolate and zucchini by hand.
- In a separate bowl, combine the flour, baking soda, salt, and cinnamon. Gradually stir flour mixture into zucchini mixture. Stir in walnuts and chocolate chips.
- Divide batter into 2 greased and floured 9 x 5-inch loaf pans.
- Bake for 1 hour, or until a toothpick inserted in the middle comes out clean. After cooling, remove from pans.

Inn on the Rio

*L*ocated on the Rio Fernando at the base of the Sangre de Cristo Mountains, just east from historic downtown Taos Plaza, the Inn on the Rio has recently been re-born. Innkeepers Robert and Julie Chahalane left the corporate "rat race" back in New England and took on the monumental task of bringing a former landmark back into its glory. Julie, with a master's degree in nutrition, knew she could satisfy her guests' hunger for healthy Southwest treats. Robert, a retired marketing executive with an background in finance and economics, knew he could make the numbers work. But what about the declining physical structures? New friends and neighbors, happy to see the interest of the new innkeepers, offered their knowledge, and the task began.

One renovation highlight is an outdoor, in-ground hot tub that offers a spectacular view of Taos Mountain during the day and the star-studded sky at night. Rooms are decorated in "cowboy casual" and "pueblo picturesque" with blankets, rugs, and art collected from all over New Mexico. Julie's new flowerbeds are filled with hollyhocks, Mexican Hats, and other native plants. The "icing on the cake" has been visits by two Southwest artists who spent several weeks painting murals on the exterior walls, arches over the doorways, and, with painstaking detail, the interiors, including each bathroom! In front of the historic Carmen Valarde Kiva fireplace in the inn's cozy gathering room, Julie offers guests suggestions for dining, sightseeing, and shopping. Robert, an outdoor enthusiast, reveals the best-kept secrets of the great outdoors for close-by hiking, mountain biking, and challenging skiing. Learn more on the Web, www.innontherio.com

Inn on the Rio

Box 6529-NDCBU
910 East Kit Carson Road
Taos, NM 87571
505-758-7199 ■ Fax 505-751-1816
Toll-free 800-859-6752

Easy Applesauce Loaf

If you're short on time, you can mix this quick bread up in a matter of minutes. If you need bread for a crowd, the recipe can easily be doubled. "Slices of Easy Applesauce Loaf make excellent sandwiches for tea when spread with whipped cream cheese," advises Innkeeper Julie Cahalane. Makes 1 loaf.

$\frac{2}{3}$ cup sugar
$\frac{1}{3}$ cup vegetable oil
  2 eggs
  2 tablespoons milk
  1 teaspoon vanilla extract
  1 cup applesauce
  2 cups flour
  1 teaspoon baking powder
$\frac{1}{2}$ teaspoon baking soda
$\frac{1}{2}$ teaspoon salt
$\frac{1}{2}$ teaspoon cinnamon
$\frac{1}{4}$ teaspoon nutmeg
$\frac{1}{2}$ cup chopped walnuts

- Preheat oven to 350 degrees. Grease a 9 x 5-inch glass loaf pan.
- With an electric mixer, beat together the sugar and oil until creamy. Beat in eggs, milk, vanilla, and applesauce. Mix well.
- In a separate bowl, sift together the flour, baking powder, baking soda, salt, cinnamon, and nutmeg.
- Add the dry ingredients to the egg mixture and incorporate. Fold in the chopped walnuts.
- Pour batter into pan. Bake for 1 hour or until a toothpick inserted in the center comes out clean.

Fairlea Farm Bed & Breakfast

*G*uests at Fairlea Farm Bed & Breakfast enjoy a spectacular view of vast pastures and the Blue Ridge Mountains. "On a clear day, if you know exactly where to look, you can even see cars in the distance along Skyline Drive in Shenandoah National Park," said Innkeeper Susan Longyear.

Fairlea Farm is a working sheep and cattle farm within two blocks of the center of the historic village of Little Washington, Virginia. George Washington surveyed and laid out plans for the village when he was 17 years old, note the Longyears. Susan and Walt opened the fieldstone manor house as a four-guestroom inn in order to share the peacefulness of the farm life with travelers.

In addition to Shenandoah National Park, plenty of attractions and activities can keep guests as busy as they like to be. Nearby are craft and antique shops, art galleries, vineyards and wineries, and Civil War battlefields. Those who love outdoor activities can visit Luray Caverns, hike, ride horses, golf, and fish close by. Learn more on the Web, www.bnb-n-va.com/fairlea.htm

Fairlea Farm Bed & Breakfast
P.O. Box 124
636 Mt. Salem Avenue
Washington, VA 22747
540-675-3679
Fax 540-675-1064

Fresh Strawberry Bread

Perfect in the height of strawberry season! If you use frozen strawberries, defrost them first and then drain well. Makes 1 loaf.

- 1½ cups flour
- ½ teaspoon baking soda
- ½ teaspoon salt
- 1 cup sugar
- ⅔ cup vegetable oil
- ½ teaspoon almond extract
- 2 eggs, well beaten
- 1¼ cups slightly mashed strawberries
- ½ cup chopped pecans

- Preheat oven to 350 degrees. Grease a 9 x 5-inch loaf pan.
- In a large bowl, sift together the flour, baking soda, and salt.
- In a separate bowl, stir together the sugar, oil, almond extract, eggs, strawberries, and pecans. Add the strawberry mixture to the flour mixture, stirring just until all ingredients are moist.
- Pour batter into pan. Bake for 60 minutes or until a toothpick inserted in the center comes out clean.

Thorwood and Rosewood Inns

*T*he year was 1983, and in Minnesota, hardly anyone had heard of B&Bs, let alone stayed in one. That was the year that Pam and Dick Thorsen opened two guestrooms in their 1880 home. They had bought the apartment building for their home and to generate a little extra income. But it turned out the Thorsens were perfect for the B&B business: Dick is quite capable of undertaking major historic restoration projects and Pam, the consummate romantic, decorates luxurious suites and entices guests to them. Today they own and operate two historic inns with a total of 15 guestrooms, and the popular inns are often named Minnesota's best and most-romantic getaways. Thorwood, as it is now named, was built as a lumber baron's home in this Mississippi rivertown. Eventually, it was turned into a private hospital and then an apartment house. After unending work, it now has seven guestrooms on three floors, all with fireplaces and/or whirlpools. In 1986, they purchased another historic home that once served as a hospital. Rosewood, owned by the city and in disrepair, was "gutted" to the studs and rebuilt with eight luxurious suites and a gift shop on the back porch. Guests can sequester themselves in luxury, ordering hat box suppers on the weekends, or breakfast served in their suites or in formal dining spaces. Or they can stroll downtown for dinner and coffee. Located only a half-hour from St. Paul, Hastings has a winery, nature center, antique stores, two coffee shops, a toy store, a Scandinavian shop, and a well-loved restaurant, all in town or nearby.

Pam, who is active in historic preservation efforts in the city, creates several special packages and theme weekends. Learn more on the Web, www.thorwoodinn.com

Thorwood and Rosewood Inns

315 Pine Street
Hastings, MN 55033
651-437-3297 ■ Fax 651-437-4129

Garlic Herb Beer Bread

"A guest of ours, a boater, shared this bread recipe," remembered Pam Thorsen, inn-keeper. *"He makes it is his little oven on his boat — there's nothing like warm bread right out of the oven, no matter where you are!"* This bread may be frozen, and makes great croutons, too! Makes 1 loaf.

1½ cups whole-wheat flour
1½ cups flour
2½ teaspoons baking powder
1½ teaspoons baking soda
 1 teaspoon dill seed
 1 teaspoon oregano
 1 teaspoon minced garlic, lightly sautéed
 1 can (12 ounces) light beer
 1 tablespoon honey

■ Preheat oven to 350 degrees. Spray a 9 x 5-inch loaf pan with non-stick cooking spray.
■ Stir together the whole-wheat flour, flour, baking powder, baking soda, dill seed, oregano, and garlic.
■ Stir in the beer and honey. Do not overmix!
■ Spoon dough into pan. Bake for 45 to 50 minutes or until a toothpick inserted in the center comes out clean.
■ Cool on rack and store covered.

Thorwood and Rosewood Inns

*T*he year was 1983, and in Minnesota, hardly anyone had heard of B&Bs, let alone stayed in one. That was the year that Pam and Dick Thorsen opened two guestrooms in their 1880 home. They had bought the apartment building for their home and to generate a little extra income. But it turned out the Thorsens were perfect for the B&B business: Dick is quite capable of undertaking major historic restoration projects and Pam, the consummate romantic, decorates luxurious suites and entices guests to them. Today they own and operate two historic inns with a total of 15 guestrooms, and the popular inns are often named Minnesota's best and most-romantic getaways. Thorwood, as it is now named, was built as a lumber baron's home in this Mississippi rivertown. Eventually, it was turned into a private hospital and then an apartment house. After unending work, it now has seven guestrooms on three floors, all with fireplaces and/or whirlpools. In 1986, they purchased another historic home that once served as a hospital. Rosewood, owned by the city and in disrepair, was "gutted" to the studs and rebuilt with eight luxurious suites and a gift shop on the back porch. Guests can sequester themselves in luxury, ordering hat box suppers on the weekends, or breakfast served in their suites or in formal dining spaces. Or they can stroll downtown for dinner and coffee. Located only a half-hour from St. Paul, Hastings has a winery, nature center, antique stores, two coffee shops, a toy store, a Scandinavian shop, and a well-loved restaurant, all in town or nearby.

Pam, who is active in historic preservation efforts in the city, creates several special packages and theme weekends. Learn more on the Web, www.thorwoodinn.com

Thorwood and Rosewood Inns

315 Pine Street
Hastings, MN 55033
651-437-3297 ■ *Fax 651-437-4129*

Goat Cheese and Sun-Dried Tomato Flatbread

Innkeeper Pam Thorsen serves this savory bread in warm wedges. Breakfast guests rave about it, especially when served with Basil Butter (in the food processor, process ½ cup soft butter, ¼ cup extra virgin olive oil and 12 large, washed fresh basil leaves until well blended). It's an especially good accompaniment to the Inns' pasta torte or egg dishes. Makes 10-12 wedges.

```
      2  cups flour
      2  teaspoons baking powder
     ¼  teaspoon baking soda
     ¼  teaspoon salt
        freshly ground black pepper
1 to 2  green onions, finely chopped
     ⅓  cup sun-dried tomatoes, packed in oil, drained and julienned
      4  ounces semi-soft goat cheese, crumbled or diced
      1  egg
½ to ⅔  cup buttermilk
```

- Preheat oven to 400 degrees. Lightly flour a large baking sheet.
- Sift flour, baking powder, baking soda and salt into a large bowl.
- Stir in a few "grinds" of black pepper, green onions, tomatoes and goat cheese Then make a "well" in the center of the mixture.
- In a small bowl, beat the egg with ½ cup buttermilk. Pour mixture into the "well."
- Using a fork, stir lightly until ingredients are just combined, adding a little more buttermilk, if necessary.
- Form dough into a rough ball and turn out onto a lightly-floured surface. Knead dough lightly 6 to 8 times, just until smooth.
- Pat dough into a ¾-inch thick circle, about 10 inches in diameter. Transfer to the floured baking sheet.
- Using a long-bladed, sharp floured knife, score the dough deeply into 10 or 12 wedges. Do not drag the knife through the dough or it will not rise evenly.
- Dust the top lightly with a little flour. Bake until risen and golden brown, 15 to 18 minutes.
- Remove from the oven and cool a bit before cutting into wedges. Serve warm with Basil Butter.

The Inn at Maplewood Farm

*L*aura and Jayme Simoes left busy lives working in a metropolitan public relations firm for life literally along a slow lane. They purchased this bucolic, picture-perfect New England farmhouse and entered careers as innkeepers. Their inn, which has welcomed visitors for two hundred years, sits on 14 acres along a winding country road, just a short drive from the town of Hillsborough. Guests looking for a quiet getaway are delighted to find that the nearest neighbors are a few cows and the 1,400-acre Fox State Forest.

Breakfast is made from locally grown and produced foods and delivered by basket to the guestrooms for a "breakfast in bed" experience. While enjoying the fireplace or rocking on the porch are the chosen daytime pursuits of many guests, there is plenty to do in the area. Laura and Jayme love directing guests to little-known antique stores, historic villages, picnic spots, and waterfalls, all within a few minutes' drive.

The Inn's four guestrooms are decorated in antiques, including an antique radio at bedside in each. Jayme's infatuation with the Golden Age of Radio has led to his own transmitter on the farm, from which he broadcasts old-time radio programs to the guestrooms via the vintage radios. Request a favorite and, chances are, he's got it in this 1,000-plus show collection. Learn more on the net at www.conknet.com/maplewoodfarm/

The Inn at Maplewood Farm
P.O. Box 1478
447 Center Road
Hillsborough, NH 03224
603-464-4242
Fax 603-464-5401
Toll-free 800-644-6695

Grandmother Jeanne's Banana Nut Bread

"This really is my Gram's favorite banana bread," notes Innkeeper Laura Simoes. *"Now it is enjoyed by guests at the inn. Gram is the best cook I know. Her food is always fabulous." Makes 1 loaf.*

- ¾ cup butter or margarine
- 1½ cups sugar
- 1½ cups mashed bananas (about 3 medium)
- 2 eggs, well beaten
- 1 teaspoon vanilla extract
- 2 cups flour, sifted
- 1 teaspoon baking soda
- ¾ teaspoon salt
- ½ cup buttermilk or sour milk
- ¾ cup chopped walnuts

- Preheat oven to 325 degrees. Grease and flour a 9 x 5-inch loaf pan.
- With an electric mixer, cream the butter and sugar. Blend in the bananas, eggs, and vanilla.
- Sift together the flour, baking soda, and salt. Add the mixture alternately with the buttermilk, mixing well after each addition.
- Add the nuts and mix thoroughly.
- Pour batter into a pan. Bake for 1¼ hours or until a toothpick inserted in the middle comes out clean.

Wild Swan Inn

*B*uilt around the turn of the century, Wild Swan is a classic example of Queen Anne–style Victorian architecture, with its ornate gingerbread and fancy finials perched on its rooftops. Painted a deep pink with green and burgundy accents, this home is typical of an age of architectural excess popular on seaside homes erected in Lewes during the heyday of the industrial era. The wraparound porch and large gazebo prominently placed at the corner of the building make it a standout among the wide variety of colonial and Victorian architecture that abounds in Lewes.

Hope and Michael Tyler, who operate Wild Swan, are self-proclaimed old house addicts. They restored an 1880s country home in northern Delaware where they lived for 25 years. After raising four children, they decided to settle in the quiet town of Lewes (est. 1861), the first town in the First State. They left careers in advertising (Michael) and state government (Hope) when they began innkeeping in January 1993.

The Tylers' antique collections include quilts, swans, door stops, and cameras. Michael often entertains guests with one of three turn-of-the-century talking machines. And, on some mornings, guests are treated to Michael's lively piano concerts on a restored 1912 player piano.

Wild Swan is within walking distance of the downtown historic district, where guests find antiques, handcrafted gifts, and fine restaurants. Lewes Beach (Delaware Bay) is a little more than a mile from the inn, and Cape Henlopen State Park (Atlantic Ocean) is only minutes away by car or on one of the inn's complimentary bicycles. The state park has 4,000 acres of clean beaches, nature trails, high dunes, and a World War II observation tower.

Wild Swan Inn
525 Kings Highway
Lewes, DE 19958
302-645-8550

Honey Banana Bread

"We've been using this breakfast quick bread recipe at Wild Swan since we opened in January 1993," said Innkeeper Mike Tyler. "Our guests really like it because it isn't heavy and overly moist like most banana bread recipes, and it isn't too sweet. Also, as an afternoon tea time item, it goes well with coffee or tea. Spreads such as fruit conserve or cream cheese go well with this bread." Here's a hint from the White Swan's kitchen: Frozen bananas work well; just thaw when ready to use. This makes them very mushy and easy to blend. Makes 1 loaf.

2¼ cups flour
1 tablespoon baking powder
½ teaspoon cinnamon
⅓ whole nutmeg, grated, or ¼ teaspoon ground nutmeg
½ teaspoon salt
⅓ cup honey
½ cup margarine
2 ounces egg substitute (or 1 egg, beaten)
1 teaspoon vanilla extract
¾ cup raisins
½ cup coarsely chopped walnuts
2 tablespoons coconut, optional
3 very ripe bananas, mashed

- Preheat oven to 350 degrees. Grease a 9 x 5 inch loaf.
- In a medium bowl, stir the flour, baking powder, cinnamon, nutmeg, and salt.
- In a separate bowl, whip the honey and margarine together until they are blended thoroughly. Add the egg substitute and vanilla, and mix well.
- Fold the raisins, nuts, and coconut into the flour mixture.
- Add about ⅓ of the mashed bananas, and about ⅓ of the egg mixture. Mix gently, and repeat, alternating banana and egg mixture only until the ingredients are blended well. "Over-mixing will make the bread tough and rubbery."
- Pour batter into pan or pans. Bake for 50 to 55 minutes or until a toothpick inserted in the middle comes out clean.
- Remove from pan, and cool on a wire rack. Rewarm slices in the microwave before serving.

Apple Gate Bed & Breakfast

_S_easonal fresh fruit is always a part of breakfast at the Apple Gate, and that includes fresh berries from a neighbor's organic farm, as well as apples, of course. Because Apple Gate is located just across the street from a ninety-acre apple orchard, Innkeeper Dianne Legenhausen chose an apple motif to decorate the inn, including naming the four guestrooms after apple varieties. Even Dianne and Ken's one hundred-pound yellow lab, Mac, is named after the Macintosh apple (the cat, Jessie, however, was acquired before the inn and has no apple ties).

Before innkeeping, Dianne taught music to elementary-age children and Ken was a police officer specializing in emergency rescues. While they had many friends in Long Island, New York, where they lived and worked for many years, they decided to head for the Monadnock region of New Hampshire, said to be picture-perfect Currier and Ives country, for their second careers as innkeepers.

They found this 1832 Colonial home just two miles from downtown Peterborough. It offered spacious accommodations for guests, including a double parlor, where guests may enjoy a fire, the library, or a TV and collection of videos. Peterborough is home to the Sharon Arts Center and the Legenhausen's bed-and-breakfast is just a few miles from the Temple Mountain and Windblown ski areas.

Apple Gate Bed & Breakfast

199 Upland Road
Peterborough, NH 03458
_603-924-6543_

Irish Soda Bread

In Dianne Legenhausen's former life, she was a teacher in Carle Place, New York. "Every year, the PTA out-did themselves to put on a luncheon for the teachers. This Irish Soda Bread was always a hit. Now it's the one that we at the Apple Gate always serve every St. Patrick's Day." Makes 2 loaves.

      4 cups flour
      ⅔ cup sugar
      2 teaspoons baking powder
      1 teaspoon baking soda
      ⅓ cup butter, cut in small chunks
   1½ cups raisins
      2 tablespoons caraway seeds
      3 eggs, beaten
      1 cup buttermilk
         milk to brush on loaves

- Preheat oven to 375 degrees. Grease a cookie sheet or 2 8-inch round cake pans.
- Sift together the flour, sugar, baking soda, and baking powder.
- With pastry fork or food processor, cut the butter into the flour mixture until it resembles fine crumbs.
- Stir in the raisins and caraway seeds.
- Combine the beaten eggs with the buttermilk. Add to dry ingredients, and stir well.
- Knead briefly, about 1 to 2 minutes, until smooth.
- Divide dough in half, and shape into 2 round loaves about 6½ inches in diameter. Place loaves on cookie sheet, or place in 2 round pans and press down to fill the pan.
- With a floured knife, cut an X about ½-inch deep through each loaf.
- Brush loaves with milk.
- Bake for 35 to 40 minutes.

Island Escape Bed & Breakfast

*G*uests at Island Escape revel in privacy — this B&B contains a single suite. The spacious accommodations include a living room finished in Hawaiian decor and a whirlpool bath. This contemporary home overlooks Puget Sound and the Olympic Mountains; a spectacular view of Mount Rainier awaits at the Fox Island bridge, just a short hike away.

Activities in this area of the Pacific Northwest run the gamut from action (scuba diving, windsurfing, sailing, mountain climbing) to total relaxation (beach-combing, bird- and wildlife-watching, reading). Nearby, the quaint fishing village of Gig Harbor hosts a myriad of events throughout the year, including parades, salmon bakes, local theatre productions, Autumn Apple Squeezing, and a summer art festival.

By concentrating on one set of guests at a time, innkeeper Paula Pascoe has found a variety of ways to pamper her visitors. Breakfast is served in the privacy of the suite; Paula features tasty, low-fat cuisine including such specialties as crab, ham, or veggie quiche, homemade granola, whole wheat huckleberry pancakes, and warm quick bread with French butter. She often strolls out to pluck fresh mint sprigs and edible flowers in season to complement the breakfast trays. E-mail address is paula@island-escape.com

Island Escape Bed & Breakfast
210 Island Blvd.
Fox Island, WA 98333
253-549-2044

Island Mango Bread

"When my husband and I lived in Hawaii," recounts Paula Pascoe, "mangoes were a plentiful island fruit. People at work would bring them in literally by the grocery sack! One of my coworkers shared this wonderfully moist recipe for making a quick bread with the mangoes. I like to present this bread with my butter shells made from imported French butter." Makes 1 loaf.

plain bread crumbs
½ cup chopped pecans, toasted
2 cups flour
2 teaspoons baking soda
1 teaspoon cinnamon
¼ teaspoon salt
⅔ cup sugar
3 eggs, beaten
1 cup vegetable oil
2 cups peeled, seeded, and finely diced mangoes (2 medium ripe mangoes)
2 teaspoons lemon juice
½ cup raisins or coconut

- Preheat oven to 350 degrees. Grease a 9 x 5-inch loaf pan and sprinkle it with plain bread crumbs.
- To toast the pecans, spread them on a cookie sheet, and toast them in a 350-degree oven until the nuts are light brown, about 8 to 10 minutes. Watch them carefully to make sure they don't burn.
- In a large bowl, sift together the flour, baking soda, cinnamon, salt, and sugar.
- In a separate bowl, stir together the eggs, oil, mangoes, and lemon juice.
- Pour the flour mixture into the mango mixture, and mix well. Stir in the nuts and raisins or coconut.
- Pour batter into pan. Bake for 40 to 45 minutes or until a toothpick inserted in the center comes out clean.
- Place pan on a cooling rack. Serve bread when cool.

Wedgwood Inns

*W*hen Carl Glassman and Dinie Silnutzer-Glassman decided to make career changes, they did their research, worked in the hospitality industry, and then threw caution to the wind. A nineteenth-century home came up for sale, one that Carl had noticed for quite some time, and they started in on the major restoration needed.

The resulting Wedgwood House, named after their collection of china, opened in 1982, just a few blocks from the village center of this historic Bucks County river town. But that was just the beginning — it turned out they enjoyed innkeeping so much, they restored other inns, and now teach classes to aspiring innkeepers, as well.

Their bed and breakfasts are nineteenth-century homes on more than two acres of landscaped grounds. Guests can enjoy the gardens, gazebo, and a game of croquet, played in traditional costume, at tea-time in the summer. In the winter, tea and treats are enjoyed fireside in the parlor.

Dinie and Carl offer fresh-baked pastries, warm comforters, a glass of homemade almond liqueur before bed, and other touches to make guests comfortable. They host a number of special events, including historic re-enactments, romantic getaways, relaxation retreats, and other events created purely for guests' enjoyment. Learn more about the inns on the Web, www.new-hope-inn.com

Wedgwood Inns
111 West Bridge Street
New Hope, PA 18938
215-862-2520
Fax 215-862-2570

Lemon Blueberry Bread

"This breakfast bread smells as good as it tastes!" Innkeeper Dinie Silnutzer-Glassman cautions that "the grated fresh lemon peel is a critical component of this recipe." Her guests rave about it each time it's served. Makes 2 loaves.

1½ cups buttermilk
3 eggs
1½ cups sugar
6 tablespoons butter
   peel of 1 lemon, grated
3 cups flour
1½ teaspoons baking soda
½ teaspoon salt
2 cups blueberries, washed and dried
¼ cup flour
   juice of 1 lemon
⅓ cup sugar

■ Preheat oven to 350 degrees. Grease a Bundt pan (or 2 9 x 5-inch loaf pans).
■ With an electric mixer, beat together the buttermilk, eggs, sugar, butter, and lemon peel.
■ In a separate bowl, combine the 3 cups flour, baking soda, and salt. Thoroughly mix the buttermilk mixture with the flour mixture.
■ In another bowl, toss the blueberries with ¼ cup flour. Gently fold the flour-coated blueberries into the batter.
■ Pour batter into pan. Bake for 1 hour (for loaf pans, test after 45 minutes with a toothpick).
■ While the bread is baking, mix together the lemon juice and sugar. When the bread is done, remove from the oven and drizzle lemon-sugar mixture over the top. Let cool.

Madelyn's in the Grove

*U*nion Grove is a small farming community at the center of seven coun-ties, in the heart of North Carolina music country. Madelyn and John Hill, proprietors of Madelyn's in the Grove, call this area in northern Iredell County "a little piece of heaven."

A day at Madelyn's in the Grove begins with a hearty gourmet breakfast, and ends with cheese and crackers, sweets, lemonade, and tea. Five unique guestrooms, cheerily decorated, promise a peaceful slumber.

Madelyn's in the Grove offers guests easy access to a wealth of musical events year round, including the annual Old Time Fiddler's Convention, the Merle Watson Festival, and a nearby "pickin' and singin' " each week. The Hills offer a variety of special weekend packages that cater to other interests as well: an Antique Getaway (including coupons, a picnic lunch, and a map to antique shops within fifty miles), a Watercolor Getaway (with artist-led classes), the popular "How to Attract Birds to Your Yard" weekend (featuring lessons in bird identification and a morning bird count), and Murder Mystery weekends.

Madelyn's in the Grove

P.O. Box 298
1836 West Memorial Highway
Union Grove, NC 28689
704-539-4151
Toll-free 800-948-4473
Fax 704-539-4080

Lemon-Lime Bread

This citrus bread is wonderful in the summer — cool and refreshing on a hot, sticky day. The sour cream and half and half make it rich and moist. Makes 2 loaves.

- 3 cups flour
- 1 cup sugar
- 1 teaspoon baking powder
- ¼ teaspoon baking soda
- 2 teaspoons finely grated lime peel
- ¾ cup sour cream
- ¾ cup half and half
- 3 eggs, beaten
- ⅓ cup vegetable oil
- 1 teaspoon lemon extract

Glaze

- 1 tablespoon water
- 2 tablespoons sugar
- juice of 2 limes

- Preheat oven to 350 degrees. Spray a 9 x 5-inch loaf pan with non-stick cooking spray and dust with flour.
- In a large bowl, sift the flour, sugar, baking powder, and baking soda. Stir in the lime peel.
- Form a well in the center of the dry ingredients. Into the well, add sour cream, half and half, eggs, and oil. Stir until well blended (do not overstir).
- Pour batter into pans and bake for 1 hour or until a toothpick inserted in the center comes out clean.
- While bread is baking, prepare the glaze. Heat water and sugar in a small bowl in the microwave until the sugar dissolves (about 1 minute). Add the lime juice. Pour over hot cake. Allow to cool and serve the next day.

White Swan Guest House

*F*rom the exquisite English country gardens that produce fruit and berries for the breakfast table, one might never guess that Innkeeper (and gardener) Peter Goldfarb moved here from Manhattan. But Peter, whose former career was interior design and contracting, has the proverbial green thumb. When combined with the Skagit Valley's fertile farmland, the result is a gorgeous garden. The fertile farmland was just about claiming this 1898 Queen Anne Victorian farmhouse when Peter found it in 1986. It was literally sinking into the ground, having fallen into disrepair in the 1940s. Using historic photos as guides, he undertook the one-year restoration himself. He transformed the farmhouse into a bright, cheery haven, with a new old-fashioned porch. Many of the rooms have views of the Cascade Mountains, Mt. Baker, and the Olympic Mountain range. The farmhouse offers three inviting guestrooms, a woodstove in the parlor, wicker chairs on the back porch, and a tempting platter of cookies waiting on the sideboard. Or guests might choose the Garden Cottage, a romantic hideaway under the trees with a private sun deck.

Peter serves a wholesome, home-cooked, Country Continental breakfast, featuring Pacific Northwest specialties, which might plenty of local fruit such as blackberries, strawberries, raspberries, and peaches. His Old-Fashioned Chocolate Chip Cookies are the guests' all-time favorite and usually are on hand to welcome guests back from their day's adventures. Guests might spend the day bike riding on the back roads, bird watching, or walking along the Skagit River, which runs in front of the house. Just a stone's throw away are the area's renown tulip fields, where thousands come every spring to see the bulb-producing fields in bloom. The towns of LaConner and Mount Vernon, with excellent shopping and dining, and the San Juan Island ferries (in Anacortes) are also nearby. Learn more on the Web, www.cnw.com/~wswan/

The White Swan Guest House

15872 Moore Road
Mount Vernon, WA 98273
360-445-6805

Lemon Pecan Bread

Innkeeper Peter Goldfarb varied a favorite Lemon Blueberry Bread recipe to make this moist tea-time treat. Increase the lemon flavor with a little lemon extract, if you like. Makes 1 loaf.

> 2 tablespoons butter, softened
> 1 egg
> 1 cup sugar
> 1 container (8-ounces) low-fat lemon yogurt
> 2 cups flour
> 1 teaspoon baking powder
> ½ teaspoon baking soda
> ½ teaspoon salt
> ½ cup chopped pecans
> sugar for topping

- Preheat oven to 350 degrees. Grease a 9 x 5-inch loaf pan.
- With an electric mixer, combine the butter, egg, sugar, and yogurt, and mix well.
- In a separate bowl, mix the flour, baking powder, baking soda, and salt.
- Add the flour mixture to the yogurt mixture, and stir just until moistened.
- Fold in the pecans.
- Pour batter into pan. Sprinkle the top with a little sugar.
- Bake for about 45 minutes, or until a toothpick inserted in the middle comes out clean. Cool on rack.

The Old Miners' Lodge

*O*ld Miners' Lodge was originally established by E. P. Ferry as lodging for single miners working his Woodside mine, located on "Treasure Mountain" behind the building. The first building, circa 1889, was two story, with dorm-style rooms, a kitchen shanty off the back, and an outhouse and blacksmith's barn behind. The Lodge was built with lumber salvaged from the surrounding mines. Electricity was added in 1912, and indoor plumbing around 1919. In the early 1920s, the Lodge was changed to married miners' housing, and converted into a number of tiny apartments.

In 1983, Hugh Daniels and Susan Wynne purchased the Lodge and surrounding property and began restoration. Hugh and Susan opened "The Old Miners' Lodge" with five guestrooms, then added two more, and then, in 1988, added a fourth section of the building, making 12 guestrooms in all. The guestrooms are all named after Park City mining era personalities, and decorated in period style. Creature comforts, such as down comforters and a hot tub under the stars, have not been overlooked. The Lodge is now owned by Jon Brinton, who built an innkeeper's cottage next door. Hugh is general manager, also overseeing the 1904 Imperior Hotel, the Lodge's sister property. Susan, Liza Simpson and Kristin Sohrweide greet guests each morning with a hearty full breakfast, fresh coffee, teas and nectars. The Lodge is in Park City's Historic District, an easy walk to Main Street shopping and dining. The Park City Mountain Resort "town lift" is a block away, and guests can ski right into the Lodge's backyard! Park City is now a year 'round resort, with horseback riding, golf, and mountain biking in the summer. Learn more on the Web, www.oldminerslodge.com

The Old Miners' Lodge
615 Woodside Avenue
P.O. Box 2639
Park City, UT 84060
435-645-8068 ■ Fax 435-645-7420

Lemon Poppyseed Tea Cake

"The tart lemon glaze for this cake sets off the delicate texture and light crunch of poppyseed," notes "kitchen goddess" Liza Simpson, who often treats guests to this wonderful breakfast bread. Makes 1 loaf.

½ cup butter
1 cup sugar
2 eggs
2 tablespoons lemon zest
2 tablespoons poppyseeds
1½ cups flour
½ teaspoon baking powder
½ teaspoon salt
½ cup milk

Glaze

3 tablespoons freshly-squeezed lemon juice
⅓ cup powdered sugar

- Preheat oven to 350 degrees. Grease a 9 x 5-inch loaf pan.
- With an electric mixer, cream the butter and sugar. Beat in eggs. Stir in lemon zest and poppyseeds.
- In a separate bowl, stir together the flour, baking powder, and salt.
- Alternately beat the flour mixture and the milk into the butter mixture.
- Turn butter into pan and bake for 45 to 50 minutes. Cool for 15 minutes in the pan.
- While bread is cooling, prepare the glaze. Combine the lemon juice and powdered sugar and stir until dissolved. Spoon over the warm loaf.
- After 15 minutes of cooling, remove the bread from pan and finish cooling on a rack.

Inn at Cedar Crossing

*A*t the Inn at Cedar Crossing, Innkeeper Terry Smith's guests are treated to a hearty continental breakfast that includes a number of wonderful creations by the Inn's pastry chef.

This Historic Register mercantile building was erected in 1884, with shops at street level and merchant's quarters upstairs. In 1985, Terry, a banker who was active in local historic preservation, purchased the building to remake into an inn. After extensive restoration, the upstairs was transformed into an inviting inn, and, later, the street level became an acclaimed restaurant with Victorian-era decor.

Today the inn has nine guestrooms with period antiques, custom-crafted poster and canopied beds, and elegant decor. Many of the guestrooms have fireplaces graced with antique mantels, double whirlpool tubs, private porches, and televisions and VCRs hidden in armoires. All of the rooms feature plump down-filled comforters and decorator fabrics, wallpapers, and linens. The Gathering Room is a relaxing spot for guests to gather by the fireplace and enjoy locally pressed apple cider, popcorn, and those homemade cookies fresh from the Inn's baking kitchen.

This Inn's restaurant has been named as one of the Top 25 restaurants in the state by the *Milwaukee Journal-Sentinel*. Open daily for all three meals, the restaurant specializes in fresh ingredients, enticingly prepared entrées, and sinful desserts, and a casual pub serves liquid refreshments. The Inn's guests head out to enjoy Door County's hiking, biking, antiquing, shopping, golfing, or just poking along the back roads of this scenic peninsula bordered by Lake Michigan. Learn more on the Web, www.innatcedarcrossing.com

Inn at Cedar Crossing
336 Louisiana Street
Sturgeon Bay, WI 54235
920-743-4200
Fax 920-743-4422

Lemon Verbena Bread

Summertime means cool Lake Michigan breezes and this lemon bread, using fresh herbs from Innkeeper Terry Smith's garden. If she doesn't have Lemon Verbena, she substitutes Lemon Balm or Lemon Thyme. See which you like best! Makes 1 loaf.

$\frac{1}{2}$ cup butter, softened
1 cup sugar
2 eggs
1$\frac{1}{4}$ cups flour
1 teaspoon baking powder
$\frac{1}{2}$ teaspoon salt
$\frac{1}{2}$ cup milk
grated peel of one lemon
1$\frac{1}{2}$ tablespoons finely chopped lemon verbena leaves

Glaze
$\frac{1}{4}$ cup powdered sugar
juice of one lemon (approximately 6 tablespoons)

- Preheat oven to 350 degrees. Grease a 9 x 5-inch loaf pan.
- With an electric mixer, cream the butter and sugar. Beat in eggs one at a time, beating well after each addition.
- In a separate bowl, sift flour, baking powder, and salt.
- Add flour mixture alternately with the milk to the butter mixture.
- Mix in lemon peel and lemon verbena or other herb.
- Pour batter into pan. Bake for 50 to 60 minutes.
- While bread is baking, combine powdered sugar and lemon juice in small saucepan. Heat just to boiling, and set aside. Brush glaze on top of loaf while bread is still hot. Cool before enjoying.

Yankee Hill Inn Bed & Breakfast

*T*he ambiance of quiet, small town life in the heart of the Kettle Moraine recreational area is what Yankee Hill Inn Bed and Breakfast Innkeepers Peg and Jim Stahlman find draws guests to their two historic homes-turned-B&Bs.

Yankee Hill Inn B&B is comprised of two historic homes restored by the Stahlmans. One is a Sheboygan County landmark, a Queen Anne Victorian–style, built in 1891. The other is an 1870 Gothic Italianate listed on the National Register of Historic Places. Both were built in the "Yankee Hill" area of Plymouth by hard-working, affluent brothers, Henry and Gilbert Huson.

Yankee Hill Inn has 12 guestrooms, decorated with period antiques and other touches to reflect historic lodging. Six guestrooms have single whirlpool tubs. Landscaped yards, parlors, fireplaces, and an enclosed front porch allow the guests to gather and relax. Each morning, guests wake up to the aroma of a full breakfast, featuring home-baked muffins and breads, and the cookie jar is open to guests.

From the Inn, guests take a short walk through Huson Park and across the Mullet River footbridge into downtown Plymouth, where they can explore charming antique and gift shops and dine in excellent restaurants. At the Plymouth Center is an art gallery, the Plymouth Historical Museum, and visitor information.

Outdoor adventures surround Plymouth in the glacially sculpted terrain. Enjoy the Kettle Moraine State Forest, many lakes, marked nature trails and the Ice Age Trail for hiking and biking. The paved Old Plank Road recreational trail, historic Plymouth walking tour, Road America race track and the Kohler Design Center, featuring the latest in Kohler bathroom and kitchen ideas, are also popular. Sheboygan and Lake Michigan are just 15 minutes away. Learn more on the Web, www.yankeehillinn.com

Yankee Hill Inn Bed & Breakfast

405 Collins Street
Plymouth, WI 53073
920-892-2222 ■ Fax 920-892-6228

Norwegian Pepper Bread

"I have no idea why this is called 'pepper' bread," said Innkeeper Peg Stahlman about this recipe, which she got from a church pamphlet more than 20 years ago. She always has some in her freezer, however, to defrost and serve "for the occasional guest who can't eat nuts." Makes 2 loaves.

> 4 cups sugar
> 2 cups milk or half and half
> 2 eggs
> 4 tablespoons melted butter
> 4 cups flour
> 1 tablespoon baking powder
> 1 tablespoon cinnamon
> 1 teaspoon ground cloves
> 1 teaspoon ginger
> ¼ teaspoon salt

- Preheat oven to 350 degrees. Grease 2 9 x 5-inch loaf pans.
- In a large bowl, beat sugar, milk, eggs and butter.
- Beat in flour, baking powder, cinnamon, cloves, ginger and salt.
- Turn dough into prepared pans and bake for at least 60 minutes or until a toothpick in the center comes out clean.

Apple Gate Bed & Breakfast

*S*easonal fresh fruit is always a part of breakfast at the Apple Gate, and that includes fresh berries from a neighbor's organic farm, as well as apples, of course. Because Apple Gate is located just across the street from a ninety-acre apple orchard, Innkeeper Dianne Legenhausen chose an apple motif to decorate the inn, including naming the four guestrooms after apple varieties. Even Dianne and Ken's one hundred-pound yellow lab, Mac, is named after the Macintosh apple (the cat, Jessie, however, was acquired before the inn and has no apple ties).

Before innkeeping, Dianne taught music to elementary-age children and Ken was a police officer specializing in emergency rescues. While they had many friends in Long Island, New York, where they lived and worked for many years, they decided to head for the Monadnock region of New Hampshire, said to be picture-perfect Currier and Ives country, for their second careers as innkeepers.

They found this 1832 Colonial home just two miles from downtown Peterborough. It offered spacious accommodations for guests, including a double parlor, where guests may enjoy a fire, the library, or a TV and collection of videos. Peterborough is home to the Sharon Arts Center, and the Legenhausen's bed-and-breakfast is just a few miles from the Temple Mountain and Windblown ski areas.

Apple Gate Bed & Breakfast
199 Upland Road
Peterborough, NH 03458
603-924-6543

Orange Apple Tea Bread

The apples for this tea bread come from the neighboring apple orchard. Dianne Legenhausen collects apple recipes to use at her inn, and this is easy and delicious, she notes. Don't bother peeling the apples! Makes 1 loaf.

  3 eggs, slightly beaten
 ½ cup vegetable oil
  1 cup sugar
  1 teaspoon orange extract
  1 teaspoon vanilla extract
  2 cups flour
  1 teaspoon baking powder
 ½ teaspoon salt
  2 apples, cored and chopped

Topping
  3 teaspoons sugar
  1 teaspoon cinnamon

- Preheat oven to 350 degrees. Grease and flour a 9 x 5-inch loaf pan.
- Whisk together the eggs, oil, sugar, orange extract, and vanilla extract until well blended.
- In a separate bowl, sift together the flour, baking powder, and salt.
- Stir the oil mixture into the flour mixture. Fold in the chopped apples.
- Pour batter into pan.
- For the topping, blend together the sugar and cinnamon; sprinkle over the batter.
- Bake for 1 hour or until a toothpick inserted in the center comes out clean.

The Old Miners' Lodge

*O*ld Miners' Lodge was originally established by E. P. Ferry as lodging for single miners working his Woodside mine, located on "Treasure Mountain" behind the building. The first building, circa 1889, was two story, with dorm-style rooms, a kitchen shanty off the back, and an outhouse and blacksmith's barn behind. The Lodge was built with lumber salvaged from the surrounding mines. Electricity was added in 1912, and indoor plumbing around 1919. In the early 1920s, the Lodge was changed to married miners' housing, and converted into a number of tiny apartments.

In 1983, Hugh Daniels and Susan Wynne purchased the Lodge and surrounding property and began restoration. Hugh and Susan opened "The Old Miners' Lodge" with five guestrooms, then added two more, and then, in 1988, added a fourth section of the building, making 12 guestrooms in all. The guestrooms are all named after Park City mining era personalities, and decorated in period style. Creature comforts, such as down comforters and a hot tub under the stars, have not been overlooked. The Lodge is now owned by Jon Brinton, who built an innkeeper's cottage next door. Hugh is general manager, also overseeing the 1904 Imperial Hotel, the Lodge's sister property. Susan, Liza Simpson and Kristin Sohrweide greet guests each morning with a hearty full breakfast, fresh coffee, teas and nectars. The Lodge is in Park City's Historic District, an easy walk to Main Street shopping and dining. The Park City Mountain Resort "town lift" is a block away, and guests can ski right into the Lodge's backyard! Park City is now a year 'round resort, with horseback riding, golf, and mountain biking in the summer. Learn more on the Web, www.oldminerslodge.com

The Old Miners' Lodge
615 Woodside Avenue
P.O. Box 2639
Park City, UT 84060
435-645-8068 ■ Fax 435-645-7420

Orange Cranberry Nut Bread

"This is one of the Lodge favorites. We serve this moist tea bread as an aprés-ski treat with assorted teas and hot cider," said Liza Simpson. "Guests say it's the perfect thing to tide them over until dinner at one of Park City's many fine restaurants." Liza suggests serving it spread with softened cream cheese. Makes 1 loaf.

1 orange
1 cup dried cranberries
2 tablespoons margarine, melted
1 teaspoon vanilla extract
1 egg, beaten
2 cups flour
¼ teaspoon baking powder
½ teaspoon baking soda
1 cup sugar
½ cup chopped almonds

- Preheat oven to 350 degrees. Grease a 9 x 5-inch loaf pan.
- Juice the orange and set juice aside in a 1 cup measuring container.
- Roughly chop and seed the orange and place the orange pieces in a food processor with the cranberries. Pulse until finely chopped. Remove mixture to a large bowl.
- Add boiling water to the juice to measure 1 cup level. Stir into orange and cranberry mixture.
- Stir in the margarine, vanilla extract, and egg.
- In another bowl, combine the flour, salt, baking powder, baking soda, and sugar. Add to the juice mixture and combine well. Stir in the nuts.
- Turn batter into pan. Bake for 40 minutes or more, until a toothpick inserted in the center comes out clean.

The Stone Hearth Inn

*G*uests of The Stone Hearth Inn awaken each day to the natural beauty of Lake Superior, the world's largest freshwater lake. This fully renovated 1920s inn cast its spell on Susan and Charlie Michels. Charlie bought the property in 1989, always having dreamt of living on "big water," and spent a year giving the rundown place a facelift, preserving original details. Susan was a guest the first month he opened; they were married a year later.

The inn's most striking feature might be its veranda, which spans the breadth of the building. Adirondack furniture invites guests to linger here, watching the waves or the calm lake, before retiring to a guestroom in the main building or in the private Boathouse or Carriage House. The Boathouse is literally perched on Superior's shore, and the Carriage House is only 40 feet from the water's edge. Three of the four guestrooms in the main lodge have lake views.

The lakeside dining room's maple hardwood flooring and hand-crafted pine furniture are the perfect backdrop for sunrises and the tantalizing smell of the Michels' unique regional cooking. Menus vary, but Charlie's specialty is blueberry wild rice pancakes; Susan's is delicately spiced French toast stuffed with cream cheese, nuts, and seasonal fruits. Local specialties also make appearances: sausage of trout or duck, northwoods maple syrup, homegrown garden produce, fresh duck eggs.

Twenty kilometers of groomed and tracked cross-country ski trails leave from the inn's front door. Visitors looking for other action spend their days exploring the Superior Hiking Trail, golfing, trout fishing, skiing, or shopping in quaint Grand Marais. An underwater trail for divers is soon to be open. A number of state parks along the "north shore" of Lake Superior offer good hiking and Superior views. Learn more on the Web, www.lakesuperior-northshore.com/stonehearth/

The Stone Hearth Inn

1118 Highway 61 East
Little Marais, MN 55614
218-226-3020 ■ Fax 218-226-3466
Toll-free 888-206-3020

Orange Pecan Pumpkin Bread

"Everyone loves this one!" Innkeeper Susan Michels loves it spread with cream cheese, or when dried fruit is added to the batter. "I developed this recipe when working in a group home right out of college, and I needed nutritious, easy recipes that made big batches!" The bread is moist and freezes well. Makes 2 loaves.

- 2½ cups sugar
- ⅔ cup butter
- 4 eggs
- 2 cups cooked pumpkin
- ¼ cup orange juice
- 3½ cups flour
- 2 teaspoons baking soda
- 1½ teaspoons nutmeg
- 1 teaspoon cinnamon
- 1 teaspoon baking powder
- ⅔ cup chopped pecans

- Preheat oven to 350 degrees. Grease and flour 2 9 x 5-inch loaf pans.
- With an electric mixer, cream the sugar and butter. Beat in the eggs, one at a time.
- Blend in pumpkin and orange juice.
- In another bowl, sift together the flour, baking soda, nutmeg, cinnamon, and baking powder. Stir into pumpkin mixture. Stir in pecans.
- Spoon batter into pans. Bake for 60 minutes or until a toothpick inserted in the center comes out clean.

Woolley Fox Bed & Breakfast

*W*oolley Fox is located in the foothills of the Laurel Highland Mountains in Ligonier, Pennsylvania. Innkeepers Barb and Wayne Carroll fell in love with the town while attending an antique show here in 1993. They immediately started looking for the perfect spot for a bed and breakfast.

They soon found this cozy country stone house, complete with two guest cottages, stone fireplaces, and a large Koi fishpond tucked into the woods, only a mile and a half from town. Unique antique furnishings and accessories, Santa Claus motifs, and classic hooked rugs are hallmarks of the Woolley Fox (the B&B takes its name from Barb's rug wools).

The Guest House and Woolley Cottage offer complete privacy, while the stone main house features an attractive guestroom, private bath, and adjacent sitting/TV area. A full country breakfast is served to guests in the main house.

Ligonier is an historic town founded in 1727. Home to Fort Ligonier, Compass Inn and Southern Alleghenies Art Museum, it's the perfect getaway place, with plenty of nearby activities and attractions in all seasons. Fallingwater and Kentuck Knob, Frank Lloyd Wright homes, are close by. E-mail address is woolley@sgi.net

Woolley Fox Bed & Breakfast
61 Lincoln Highway East
Ligonier, PA 15658
724-238-3004

Papaya Crunch Bread

This is a sweet, moist bread with a little crunch to each bite. Papaya Crunch Bread can be made a day ahead. Makes 1 loaf.

⅓ cup butter
⅔ cup sugar
2 eggs
¼ cup orange juice
1 teaspoon orange extract
½ cup sour cream
½ cup milk
1½ cups flour
1 teaspoon baking soda
½ teaspoon salt
1 papaya, peeled, seeded, and chopped
2 tablespoons grated orange peel
1⅓ cups any corn and wheat flake cereal, such as Post's Honey Bunches of Oats™
sugar for topping

- Preheat oven to 350 degrees. Grease or spray a 9 x 5-inch loaf pan with non-stick cooking spray.
- With an electric mixer, cream the butter and sugar. Beat in the eggs; then blend in the orange juice and orange extract.
- In a separate bowl, whisk together the sour cream and milk.
- In another bowl, stir together the flour, baking soda, and salt.
- Add the dry ingredients alternately with the sour cream mixture to the butter mixture, mixing until just blended.
- By hand, stir in the chopped papaya, orange peel, and cereal until just mixed.
- Pour batter into pan. Sprinkle sugar on top.
- Bake for 1 hour or until a toothpick inserted in the center comes out clean.

The Lamplighter
Bed & Breakfast

*J*udy and Heinz Bertram and their cocker spaniel, Freddy, welcome recreational and business travelers to their Queen Anne–style home, which was built in 1895 by a local doctor as his home and office. After living for more than twenty years in Germany and traveling extensively throughout Europe, the Bertrams brought their collection of fine antiques and original paintings and lithographs to their Michigan B&B.

They purchased their "dream B&B" virtually overnight, Judy said. She and Heinz added a deck with a gazebo and a red brick patio and extensive landscaping so that summer guests can enjoy refreshments outside. Judy is a Michigan native and former administrator in the Department of Defense school system overseas, and Heinz, originally from Germany, is a retired U.S. Air Force officer.

Breakfast may be served on the patio, in the gazebo, or in the formal dining room, depending on the season. Afterwards, guests might head off to swim in Lake Michigan, stroll along its miles of sandy beaches, walk to the lighthouse at the entrance to Ludington harbor, or shop for antiques. Guests find plenty of outdoor activities year 'round, including biking through Ludington State Park, rated one of the state's best, skiing on miles of groomed cross-country trails, or hiking or strolling along nature trails. Judy and Heinz are happy to help guests plan their itinerary to explore scenic Western Michigan. Learn more on the Web, www.laketolake.com/lamplighter

The Lamplighter
602 East Ludington Avenue
Ludington, MI 49431
616-843-9792
Fax 616-845-6070

Peach Almond Yogurt Bread

"This bread can be frozen and is a lifesaver for a last-minute addition to the breakfast menu," Innkeeper Judy Bertram said. "Take them out the night before and zap them in the microwave for 15 seconds just before cutting and serving for that freshly baked taste." Makes 2 loaves.

>   3 cups flour
>   1 teaspoon salt
>   1 teaspoon baking soda
>   ½ teaspoon baking powder
>   3 eggs
>   1 cup vegetable oil
> 1½ cups sugar
>   2 cups peach yogurt
>   1 tablespoon almond extract
>   ½ cup sliced almonds, optional

- Preheat oven to 325 degrees. Grease 2 9 x 5-inch loaf pans.
- In a large bowl, sift together the flour, salt, baking soda, and baking powder.
- In a separate large bowl, lightly beat the eggs. Pour in the oil and sugar, and beat well. Mix in the yogurt and almond extract.
- Stir the egg mixture into the dry ingredients. Stir in the nuts, if desired. Mix until just combined.
- Pour batter into pans. Bake for about 45 minutes or until a toothpick inserted in the middle comes out clean.

Island Escape Bed & Breakfast

*G*uests at Island Escape revel in privacy — this B&B contains a single suite. The spacious accommodations include a living room finished in Hawaiian decor and a whirlpool bath. This contemporary home overlooks Puget Sound and the Olympic Mountains; a spectacular view of Mount Rainier awaits at the Fox Island bridge, just a short hike away.

Activities in this area of the Pacific Northwest run the gamut from action (scuba diving, windsurfing, sailing, mountain climbing) to total relaxation (beach-combing, bird- and wildlife-watching, reading). Nearby, the quaint fishing village of Gig Harbor hosts a myriad of events throughout the year, including parades, salmon bakes, local theatre productions, Autumn Apple Squeezing, and a summer art festival.

By concentrating on one set of guests at a time, innkeeper Paula Pascoe has found a variety of ways to pamper her visitors. Breakfast is served in the privacy of the suite; Paula features tasty, low-fat cuisine including such specialties as crab, ham, or veggie quiche, homemade granola, whole-wheat huckleberry pancakes, and warm quick bread with French butter. She often strolls out to pluck fresh mint sprigs and edible flowers in season to complement the breakfast trays. E-mail address is paula@island-escape.com

Island Escape Bed & Breakfast
210 Island Blvd.
Fox Island, WA 98333
253-549-2044

Pecan Prune Bread

Paula Pascoe has had this recipe since she was in collage and spent Thanksgiving with a friend, whose mother made this bread. This is a delicious and high-fiber breakfast quick bread that she makes in four mini-loaf pans. "We like to wrap and store the loaves in the refrigerator for one day before serving to enhance the flavors," Paula said. Makes 2 loaves.

    plain bread crumbs
3 cups flour
1 teaspoon salt
1 teaspoon baking soda
1 teaspoon baking powder
1 teaspoon cinnamon
1 teaspoon nutmeg
1 teaspoon allspice
1 teaspoon ground cloves
¾ cup vegetable oil
1½ cups sugar
3 eggs
1 cup buttermilk
1 cup moist-pack pitted prunes, cut into ½-inch pieces with clean kitchen shears
1 cup chopped pecans

- Preheat oven to 350 degrees. Grease 2 9 x 5-inch loaf pans and sprinkle with bread crumbs.
- In a large bowl, sift together the flour, salt, baking soda, baking powder, and spices.
- With an electric mixer, cream the oil and sugar until smooth. Add the eggs, and mix thoroughly.
- Add the flour mixture alternately with the buttermilk to the batter. With the last addition of the flour mixture, add the prunes and nuts. Be sure the batter is well blended.
- Spoon the batter into the pans. Bake for 45 minutes or until a toothpick inserted in the center comes out clean. Turn out onto cooling racks.

The Doanleigh Inn

*T*he Doanleigh Inn, Kansas City's first B&B, was named after one of the original innkeeper's great-great-great grandmothers, Sarah Doanleigh of Wales. The current innkeepers, Cynthia Brogdon and Terry Maturo, purchased the grand inn in 1985 and have begun extensive renovations of the 1907 Georgian mansion, once a majestic private home.

The couple's interest in innkeeping began after Cynthia spent several years traveling throughout the country on business. Tiring of hotels and seeking more personalized service in a relaxed atmosphere, she began staying in B&Bs and country inns. Today, as innkeepers, Cynthia and Terry try to offer the service and pampering for their business and leisure guests that they would appreciate themselves. Computer modem access in guestrooms, early breakfasts, in-room speaker phones, and other conveniences are all efforts to meet the needs of business travelers. And, while the breakfast may be served as early as 6:00 in the morning, it is still delicious gourmet fare that has earned Cynthia quite a reputation. Guests enjoy evening hors d'oeuvres and wine, as well.

In the heart of Kansas City, the Doanleigh Inn overlooks historic Hyde Park, just 12 minutes from downtown. It is closer still to the famed Country Club Plaza, Hallmark Crown Center, and the University of Missouri, and it is near the Nelson-Atkins Museum of Art and other attractions. Learn more on the Web, www.doanleigh.com

The Doanleigh Inn
217 East 37th Street
Kansas City, MO 64111
816-753-2667
Fax 816-531-5185

Pineapple Yogurt Bread

"This bread gets rave reviews!" reported Innkeeper Cynthia Brogdon. "It is very moist and flavorful. It has become one of our most-requested breads by repeat guests." Makes 1 Bundt cake.

> 1 cup butter
> 2 cups sugar
> 5 eggs
> 1 teaspoon vanilla extract
> 3 cups flour
> 1 teaspoon baking powder
> ¼ teaspoon baking soda
> 1 container (8 ounces) pineapple yogurt
> 1 can (8 ounces) crushed pineapple

- Preheat oven to 325 degrees. Grease and flour a Bundt pan.
- With an electric mixer, beat the butter and sugar until light and fluffy. Beat in the vanilla extract. Add the eggs, 1 at a time, beating after each addition.
- In a separate bowl, stir together the flour, baking powder, and baking soda. Add the flour mixture alternately with the yogurt to the butter mixture.
- Stir in the pineapple by hand.
- Pour batter into pan. Bake for 65 minutes or until a toothpick inserted in the center comes out clean. Cool and then invert to remove from pan.

Justin Trails Country Inn

A third-generation dairy farm, the Justin Trails Country Inn property has been in the Justin family since 1914. In 1985, Don and Donna Justin opened ten kilometers of cross-country ski trails, and the B&B opened a year later. The award-winning Justin Trails is set among the scenic wooded hills and valleys of southwestern Wisconsin, near Sparta. The cozy 1920s farmhouse with four guestrooms is complemented by three private luxury cottages: the Granary, the Little House on the Prairie, and the Paul Bunyan — the last two are log cabins. All the rooms are decorated in a romantic country style with such special touches as hand-crafted log furnishings, Amish hickory rocking chairs, stone fireplaces, and painted pine floors.

Donna treats her guests, hungry from the previous day's worth of outdoor activities, to a four-course breakfast that features homemade muffins, granola, yogurt, applesauce or fresh fruit, an entrée, and of course coffee, tea, and juice. A recent addition at Justin Trails is The Eatery, featuring gourmet regional and vegetarian cuisine and a cozy conversation area. But that will soon be turned into something else because the Justins are converting the dairy barn to serve as the restaurant and additional lodging. Area attractions include 12½ kilometers of private, groomed cross-country ski trails, snowtubing, snowshoeing, hiking, biking on the Elroy-Sparta Trail, canoeing, and visiting the nearby Amish community, state and national parks and forests, and quaint antique shops. Guests are encouraged to play with the rabbits, kittens, Peter the pygmy goat, and chickens. The Justins offer special weekend getaways throughout the year, such as family fun packages, ski fests, and women's retreats. Learn more on the Web, www.justintrails.com

Justin Trails Country Inn
7452 Kathryn Avenue on Co. J
Sparta, WI 54656
608-269-4522 ■ Fax 608-269-3280
Toll-free 800-488-4521

Pumpkin Chocolate-Covered Raisin Bread

"This is a great recipe to make the day or two ahead of time for guests who want an early breakfast. This is a very moist bread that slices better after a couple of days wrapped in plastic wrap," explains Innkeeper Donna Justin. Makes 2 Bundt-shaped loaves.

　　1　can (16 ounces) pumpkin
　　1　cup vegetable oil
　　2　eggs
　1½　cups brown sugar, packed
　1½　cups sugar
　1½　teaspoons cinnamon
　　3　teaspoons minced fresh ginger
　　½　teaspoon mace
　3⅓　cups flour
　　2　teaspoons baking soda
　　1　cup chopped pecans
　　1　cup chocolate-covered raisins

Filling
　　8　ounces cream cheese, softened
　　⅓　cup sugar
　　1　tablespoon flour
　　1　egg
　　2　teaspoons grated orange peel

- Preheat oven to 325 degrees. Grease and flour 2 Bundt pans.
- With an electric mixer, combine the pumpkin, oil, and eggs, and mix well. Add the brown sugar, sugar, cinnamon, fresh ginger, mace, flour, and baking soda. Stir in the pecans and chocolate-covered raisins.
- To make the filling, beat together the cream cheese, sugar, and flour. Beat in the egg. Stir in the orange peel.
- Pour ¼ of the batter into each of the two pans. Carefully spread the filling over the batter (½ of the filling in each pan). Cover filling with the remaining batter.
- Bake for 1½ hours, or until a toothpick inserted in the middle comes out clean.
- Cool for 10 minutes before removing. Plastic-wrap bread to store in refrigerator.

Chambered Nautilus

*I*n May 1996, longtime Seattle residents Joyce Schulte and Steven Poole changed careers and became the third owners to welcome guests to this gracious inn. Built in 1915 by University of Washington professor Dr. Herbert Gowen and his wife, Anne, this elegant 1915 Georgian Colonial home perches on a peaceful hill in Seattle's University district. In the mid 1980s, the home was turned into a B&B. Joyce and Steve are collectors of antique oak furniture and several new pieces have been added to the collection. Recent remodeling projects have dressed up the inn by refinishing hardwood floors, adding and updating bathrooms, and remodeling an attic room to include a fireplace.

Chambered Nautilus offers six large, airy guestrooms, each outfitted with antiques and down comforters. Fresh flowers, bottled water, soft robes, and teddy bears welcome guests to each room, several of which overlook the gardens and the stunning Cascade Mountains. Guests are welcome to relax by the fire in the living room, indulging in fresh-baked cookies on the sunporch or in the garden, or delving into the extensive library. Breakfast is served in the elegant dining room or on the sunporch. Steve prepares the sumptuous meal, which includes fresh fruit, juice, granola, baked treats, and such unique entrées as Northwest Breakfast Pie. Of course, there's always plenty of fresh-roasted Seattle coffee! Guests will find plenty to do in the area. Downtown, visit the Pike Place Market, the Seattle Aquarium, the Klondike Gold Rush National Historical Park, or ride the ferries or the monorail. Wineries, waterfalls, the Woodland Park Zoo, restaurants, and plenty of outdoor recreation is also found in the area. Nearby is the Burke-Gilman trail for bikers and walkers and Ravenna Park. Learn more on the Web, www.chamberednautilus.com

Chambered Nautilus
5005 22nd Avenue NE
Seattle, WA 98105
206-522-2536 ■ *Fax 206-528-0898*

Pumpkin Spice Bread

Innkeeper Joyce Schulte discovered this old family recipe was perfect for a new innkeeper. It's quick to make, freezes well, makes three large loaves, and tastes great. "It is one of the most popular items in the early breakfast baskets that we make for our business travelers with early morning appointments," she said. Makes 3 loaves.

> 3 cups flour
> $3\frac{1}{2}$ cups sugar
> $1\frac{1}{2}$ teaspoons cinnamon
> $1\frac{1}{2}$ teaspoons nutmeg
> $1\frac{1}{2}$ teaspoons salt
> 2 teaspoons baking soda
> 1 cup corn oil (not canola or vegetable oil)
> $\frac{2}{3}$ cup water
> 4 eggs
> 1 can (16 ounces) pumpkin
> $1\frac{1}{2}$ cups chopped walnuts

- Preheat oven to 350 degrees. Grease and liberally flour 3 9 x 5-inch loaf pans.
- In a large bowl, mix together the flour, sugar, cinnamon, nutmeg, salt, and baking soda.
- Add the corn oil, water, eggs, and pumpkin. Mix well with an electric mixer. Stir in nuts.
- Pour into pans. Bake for 1 hour, or until toothpick inserted in middle comes out clean.

Thorwood and Rosewood Inns

*T*he year was 1983, and in Minnesota, hardly anyone had heard of B&Bs, let alone stayed in one. That was the year that Pam and Dick Thorsen opened two guestrooms in their 1880 home. They had bought the apartment building for their home and to generate a little extra income. But it turned out the Thorsens were perfect for the B&B business: Dick is quite capable of undertaking major historic restoration projects and Pam, the consummate romantic, decorates luxurious suites and entices guests to them. Today they own and operate two historic inns with a total of 15 guestrooms, and the popular inns are often named Minnesota's best and most-romantic getaways. Thorwood, as it is now named, was built as a lumber baron's home in this Mississippi rivertown. Eventually, it was turned into a private hospital and then an apartment house. After unending work, it now has seven guestrooms on three floors, all with fireplaces and/or whirlpools. In 1986, they purchased another historic home that once served as a hospital. Rosewood, owned by the city and in disrepair, was "gutted" to the studs and rebuilt with eight luxurious suites and a gift shop on the back porch. Guests can sequester themselves in luxury, ordering hat box suppers on the weekends, or breakfast served in their suites or in formal dining spaces. Or they can stroll downtown for dinner and coffee. Located only a half-hour from St. Paul, Hastings has a winery, nature center, antique stores, two coffee shops, a toy store, a Scandinavian shop, and a well-loved restaurant, all in town or nearby.

Pam, who is active in historic preservation efforts in the city, creates several special packages and theme weekends. Learn more on the Web, www.thorwoodinn.com

Thorwood and Rosewood Inns

315 Pine Street
Hastings, MN 55033
651-437-3297 ■ Fax 651-437-4129

Raisin Beer Bread

A guest who spent a lot of time cooking on a small boat gave this recipe to Innkeeper Pam Thorsen. This bread tastes wonderful and easily baked in his small boat oven. Pam notes the coarse bread (which does not taste like beer, by the way) makes wonderful French toast. She prefers to use a corn-based beer. Makes 1 loaf.

1½ cups whole-wheat flour
1½ cups flour
2½ teaspoons baking powder
1½ teaspoons baking soda
1 teaspoon cinnamon
½ teaspoon nutmeg
⅛ teaspoon ground cloves
½ cup raisins (or dried cranberries)
1 can (12 ounces) light beer
1 tablespoon honey

- Preheat oven to 350 degrees. Spray a 9 x 5-inch pan with cooking spray.
- In a large bowl, combine the whole-wheat flour, flour, baking powder, baking soda, cinnamon, nutmeg, cloves, and raisins.
- Stir in the beer and honey. Do not overmix!
- Spoon dough into prepared pan and bake for 45 to 50 minutes or until a toothpick inserted in the middle comes out clean.
- Cool on rack and store covered.

The Settlement at Round Top

*L*arry and Karen Beever's Settlement at Round Top is an historical treasure set on 35 acres in the lush green, gently rolling hills of east central Texas. "We strive to make it a place where guests can enjoy times past in the ease of today's comfort," Karen said.

The innkeepers spent their honeymoon in Europe and fell in love with the bed and breakfast concept. "It was just natural that when we found a Civil War-era homestead so run down that our realtor refused to show it to us, that we ultimately decided to share our restored treasure," Karen said. They also brought in additional pioneer log cabins and cottages scheduled to be torn down. Their renovation and restoration efforts have turned them into antique-filled guest accommodations with fireplaces, whirlpools and porches.

A large notched and pegged Civil War-era barn is the unique setting for the full breakfasts, served with a flare by Larry and Karen. The barn also is available for conferences and retreats. The setting is full of deer, birds, miniature roses, centuries-old oak trees, split rail fences, miniature horses, and, in season, the wildflowers for which Texas is famous. Karen and Larry are active members of the Historic Accommodations of Texas and the prestigious Independent Innkeepers Association and the Settlement was featured in the June 1997 *Country Living Magazine*. Learn more on the Web, www.thesettlement.com

The Settlement at Round Top

P.O. Box 176
Round Top, TX 78954
409-249-5015
Fax 409-249-5587
Toll-free 888-ROUNDTOP

Rhubarb Nut Bread

"Coming from a large family in North Dakota, we looked forward to the warm days of summertime, and the lush rhubarb stalks growing next to the barn," recalled Innkeeper Karen Beevers. She and her siblings enjoyed the tart stems in bread, pies or raw, sprinkled with sugar! Makes 2 loaves.

- 1½ cups brown sugar, packed
- ⅔ cup vegetable oil
- 1 egg
- 1 teaspoon baking soda
- 1 teaspoon salt
- 1 teaspoon vanilla extract
- 1 cup sour milk
- 2½ cups flour
- 1½ cups diced rhubarb
- ½ cups chopped nuts

Topping
- ½ cup brown sugar, packed
- 1 tablespoon butter

- ■ Preheat oven to 325 degrees. Grease 2 9 x 5-inch loaf pans.
- ■ With an electric mixer, beat together the brown sugar, oil, and egg.
- ■ In a separate bowl, combine the baking soda, salt, vanilla, and sour milk. Stir the milk mixture into the egg mixture.
- ■ Stir in the flour, rhubarb, and nuts.
- ■ Pour batter into pans.
- ■ To make the topping, coarsely blend ½ cup brown sugar with 1 tablespoon butter. Sprinkle on top of the batter.
- ■ Bake for 1 hour, or until a toothpick inserted in the middle comes out clean.

Angel Arbor
Bed & Breakfast Inn

*V*eteran Houston Innkeeper Marguerite Swanson, with her husband, Dean, opened Angel Arbor Bed & Breakfast Inn in September 1995 after a busy six-month restoration. Marguerite successfully operated Durham House B&B Inn, just a half-block away, for ten years before "downsizing" to this slightly smaller Georgian-style home. Both homes were once owned by Jay L. Durham, a Houston Heights benefactor. As father of eight, he aspired to acquire a house for each of his children, but he fell short of that goal because of the Great Depression.

Marguerite, a San Antonio native, easily moved into innkeeping as a profession. "I came from a big family and I was used to entertaining, and I just loved the idea of having people in my house all the time," she said. "I never have a day when I wake up and wish I were doing something else." Durham House quickly established a reputation for gracious accommodations and special occasions, such as unique murder mystery dinners, teas, showers, and small private parties.

In order to have more free time, she and Dean bought the elegant red brick residence that is now the Angel Arbor. It has five spacious guestrooms upstairs, three of which have double whirlpool tubs. The 1923 home, built for Katherine and John McTighe, had most recently been used for offices. The Swansons removed glued-down carpet, refinished the original hardwood floors, installed new bathrooms, and replaced many fixtures. They turned the screened porch into a year-round solarium overlooking the garden, with Marguerite's favorite angel statue and Dean's favorite vine-covered arbor. Guests enjoy the garden as well as the first-floor parlor, solarium, sunroom, and dining room. Learn more on the Web, www.angelarbor.com

Angel Arbor Bed & Breakfast Inn
848 Heights Boulevard
Houston, TX 77007
713-868-4654 ■ Toll-free 800-722-8788
Fax 713-861-3189

Rum Raisin Bread

This is a raisin bread for people who think they don't like raisins, said Marguerite Swanson. "I got the idea for using golden raisins from a guest who once told me she didn't like looking at 'all those dark things' in her breakfast bread." Makes 1 loaf.

½ cup rum
1 cup golden raisins
1 teaspoon vanilla extract
  peel of 1 lemon, grated
2 cups flour
¾ cup sugar
2 teaspoons baking powder
½ teaspoon baking soda
½ teaspoon salt
¼ teaspoon nutmeg
2 eggs
½ cup sour cream
¼ cup butter, melted
  powdered sugar, optional

■ Preheat oven to 350 degrees. Grease a 9 x 5-inch loaf pan.
■ In a medium bowl, stir together the rum, raisins, vanilla, and lemon peel.
■ In a separate bowl, thoroughly mix together the flour, sugar, baking powder, baking soda, salt, and nutmeg.
■ In a smaller bowl, whisk together the eggs, sour cream, and butter. Pour into the flour mixture.
■ Mix egg-flour mixture with the rum-raisin mixture, and fold in just until combined.
■ Pour batter into pan. Bake for 50 minutes, or until a toothpick inserted in the middle comes out clean.
■ Cool bread on a wire rack, and dust with powdered sugar, if desired.

Watch Hill Bed & Breakfast

*W*hen guests come to Barbara Lauterbach's B&B, they may come for many reasons — but when they come *back*, "food" is always one that draws them. A gourmet chef, Barbara trained at renowned culinary institutes in Paris, Italy, and England. Her food-related career has included developing cooking schools for a chain of department stores, serving as an instructor at the New England Culinary Institute, and acting as a consultant and spokesperson for food-related businesses. She also has done regular television cooking segments and presents classes around the country. When she bought the B&B in 1989, her background was just one of the talents that made innkeeping attractive to her. Guests love to sit and chat during an excellent breakfast, and Barbara holds cooking classes at the B&B.

Watch Hill is one of the oldest homes in Center Harbor. Built circa 1772 by the brother of the town's founder, it has views of Lake Winnipesaukee, just down the street. Guests in the four guestrooms especially enjoy the home's porch in the summer or warming up with a mug of hot cider after skiing or snowmobiling in the winter. Barbara's full country breakfast often showcases New Hampshire products and may feature fresh, hot breads, sausage, bacon, home-fries, fresh fruit, and brown eggs. Guests enjoy the food and the conversation, which often turns to the how her B&B was named (after the champion bull mastiffs Barbara used to raise from the Watch Hill kennel in Cincinnati, Ohio). Watch Hill is a five-minute walk from one of the country's foremost quilt shops, and quilters are frequent guests. "Sometimes they come in vans and take over the whole place!" Barbara said. "They have Show and Tell in the evening, inspecting each other's purchases of fabrics and patterns."

Watch Hill Bed & Breakfast

P.O. Box 1605
Center Harbor, NH 03226
603-253-4334
Fax 603-253-8560

Savory Christmas Bread

Innkeeper Barbara Lauterbach recommends that when you serve Savory Christmas Bread, cut it into very thin slices and fan them onto a plate. Eat as is, or spread with butter or herb butter. Fresh chives or the green part of scallions may be substituted for the green pepper, and drained pimentos or chopped red bell pepper may be substituted for the sundried tomatoes. Makes 1 loaf.

3 cups flour
2 teaspoons baking powder
1 teaspoon salt
8 ounces provolone cheese, grated (approximately 2 cups)
4 eggs, beaten
½ cup evaporated milk
3 large garlic cloves, crushed
¼ cup chopped green pepper
¼ cup chopped sun-dried tomatoes

- Preheat oven to 350 degrees. Grease a cookie sheet.
- In a large bowl, mix the flour, baking powder, salt, and cheese. Add the beaten eggs, reserving 2 tablespoons for glazing the bread before baking.
- Mix in the evaporated milk, garlic, green pepper, and sun-dried tomatoes, stirring to make a soft dough.
- Turn the dough out on a well-floured surface and form it into a smooth ball. Roll the ball into a log shape about 10 inches long. Place on cookie sheet. Brush with reserved beaten egg.
- Bake for about 30 to 35 minutes, or until the loaf is golden brown. Cool thoroughly before serving.

The Doanleigh Inn

*T*he Doanleigh Inn, Kansas City's first B&B, was named after one of the original innkeeper's great-great-great grandmothers, Sarah Doanleigh of Wales. The current innkeepers, Cynthia Brogdon and Terry Maturo, purchased the grand inn in 1985 and have begun extensive renovations of the 1907 Georgian mansion, once a majestic private home.

The couple's interest in innkeeping began after Cynthia spent several years traveling throughout the country on business. Tiring of hotels and seeking more personalized service in a relaxed atmosphere, she began staying in B&Bs and country inns. Today, as innkeepers, Cynthia and Terry try to offer the service and pampering for their business and leisure guests that they would appreciate themselves. Computer modem access in guestrooms, early breakfasts, in-room speaker phones, and other conveniences are all efforts to meet the needs of business travelers. And, while the breakfast may be served as early as 6:00 in the morning, it is still delicious gourmet fare that has earned Cynthia quite a reputation. Guests enjoy evening hors d'oeuvres and wine, as well.

In the heart of Kansas City, the Doanleigh Inn overlooks historic Hyde Park, just 12 minutes from downtown. It is closer still to the famed Country Club Plaza, Hallmark Crown Center, and the University of Missouri, and it is near the Nelson-Atkins Museum of Art and other attractions. Learn more on the Web, www.doanleigh.com

The Doanleigh Inn

217 East 37th Street
Kansas City, MO 64111
816-753-2667
Fax 816-531-5185

Sour Cream Raisin Bread

"This is a very moist raisin bread. It's very simple to make, and the results are outstand-ing! You can also make a low-fat version of this bread," says Cynthia Brogdon, innkeeper. Just substitute nonfat sour cream for the "real stuff," ½ cup vegetable oil for the butter, and ½ cup egg substitute for the eggs. Makes 1 loaf.

1½ cups sour cream (low-fat is okay)
1½ teaspoons baking soda
 ½ cup unsalted butter, melted
  1 cup sugar
  2 eggs
  1 cup raisins
1½ cups flour
  2 teaspoons baking powder
  3 teaspoons cinnamon
 ½ teaspoon salt
 ½ cup brown sugar, packed
  2 tablespoons pure maple syrup
 ½ cup chopped walnuts

■ Preheat oven to 350 degrees. Grease a 9 x 5-inch loaf pan.
■ In a large bowl, stir together the sour cream and baking soda. Set aside for 5 minutes.
■ To the sour cream mixture, whisk in the melted butter, sugar, eggs, and raisins. Set aside.
■ In a small bowl, stir together the flour, baking powder, 1 teaspoon of the cinnamon, and salt. Add to the sour cream mixture, and stir just until blended. Spread half of the batter into pan.
■ Stir together the remaining 2 teaspoons cinnamon, brown sugar, maple syrup, and walnuts. Sprinkle this mixture over the batter in the pan. Cover with the remaining batter.
■ Bake for about 65 to 75 minutes, or until a toothpick inserted in the middle comes out clean.
■ Cool in the pan for 15 minutes; then turn out onto a wire rack to cool com-pletely.

Claddagh Inn

"*F*riendship, love and loyalty" — the meaning of the Claddagh, a Gaelic symbol that consists of two hands, a heart and a crown — is the tradition followed at Gerri and Augie Emanuele's inn. "We greet and serve guests each morning with a warm smile and hearty breakfast," said Gerri, who bought this operating 14 guestroom-inn with her husband in 1996. Breakfast is served in the dining room, and it might start with imported Irish oatmeal, then be followed with a variety of homemade breads and one special main dish each day.

The exact date the Inn was built is unknown, but the "Smith-Green House," as it was called, was built by W.A. Smith between 1888 and 1906. In 1906, Elsie Sindorf bought it and opened The Charleston Boarding House to accommodate the large numbers of Charlestonians coming to Hendersonville to escape the humid summers. After several different owners, the Carberry's purchased it in 1985, closed it, renovated it, and opened the town's first Bed & Breakfast.

Many guests start and end their day on the large verandah, where porch rockers beckon guests to slow down and put their feet up. Indoors, guests are welcome to use the parlor and library. Pleasant conversation and a little sherry, served in the library, are sometimes accompanied by impromptu piano-playing as a bedtime send-off.

Just blocks from the historical downtown, the Claddagh Inn is ideally located to serve as a home base for a Western Carolina getaway. Many restaurants, antique and gift shops, local craft studios and attractions are within walking distance of that inviting front porch. Day trip destinations include the Biltmore Estate, Chimney Rock, Carl Sandburg's home, Pisgah National Forest and the Flat Rock Playhouse. Learn more on the Web, www.claddaghinn.com

Claddagh Inn
755 North Main Street
Hendersonville, NC 28792
828-697-7778 ■ Fax 828-697-8664

Strawberry Bread

"This recipe is always requested," notes Innkeeper Gerri Emanuele. "If there is any bread left after breakfast, we always wrap it up for one of the guests who is checking out to take along in the car for a snack. It is never refused, and they get to take a little reminder of their stay at our Inn along with them for the ride." Makes 2 loaves.

      3 cups flour
      1 teaspoon baking soda
      1 teaspoon salt
      1 teaspoon cinnamon
      2 cups sugar
      4 eggs, beaten
      2 cups fresh strawberries (smaller ones whole, larger ones sliced)
   1½ cups vegetable oil
      1 cup chopped nuts, optional

- Preheat oven to 325 degrees. Grease 2 9 x 5-inch loaf pans.
- In a large bowl, sift together the flour, baking soda, salt, cinnamon, and sugar.
- In a separate bowl, combine the eggs, strawberries, and oil. Stir in the nuts. Gently combine the strawberry mixture with the flour mixture.
- Pour batter into pans. Bake for 1 hour or until a toothpick inserted in the center comes out clean.

Window on the Winds

*L*eanne McClain's two-story log home is the perfect base for a Wyoming vacation. The second floor, with four guestrooms featuring lodgepole pine beds, is reserved for guests. A view of the Wind River Mountains from the fireside gathering room has been known to take more than one guest's breath away.

Leanne is an archeologist who enjoys sharing her perspective on the area and can offer information about the history of the Green River Basin and the Wind River Range. She is also happy to help guests plan their fishing, rafting, riding, skiing, or hiking adventures.

Window on the Winds is located directly on the Continental Divide Snowmobile Trail at elevation 7,175 feet. A guided inn-to-inn snowmobile tour that leads into Yellowstone National Park leaves right from the property. Guests can snowmobile from the front door, through the Wind River Mountains and on into Yellowstone National Park. Other winter adventures include dog sledding and racing, and both cross-country and downhill skiing.

Whatever the season, guests can return from a day of outdoor adventure to relax and enjoy the hot tub. Fresh fruits, vegetables, and whole grains are always on the breakfast menu. Leanne specializes in western hospitality, even offering to board guests' horses. The bed and breakfast is within a two-hour drive of Jackson Hole and the Grand Teton and Yellowstone National Parks. Learn more on the Web, www.cruising-america.com/windowonwinds

Window on the Winds Bed & Breakfast

10151 Highway 191, P.O. Box 996
Pinedale, WY 82941
307-367-2600
Fax 307-367-2395
Toll-free 888-367-1345

Whole-Wheat Mountain Cranberry Bread

"I first started making this bread for Thanksgiving," said Innkeeper Leanne McClain. "The cranberries in it are really pretty and festive when it is sliced." But because fresh cranberries freeze so well, she now makes it year 'round. The hearty, healthy ingredients provide extra energy for her outdoors-loving guests. Makes 2 small loaves.

- ¼ cup butter or margarine
- ⅔ cup honey
- 2 eggs
- 1 cup orange juice
- 2 cups whole-wheat flour
- ⅓ cup instant dry milk
- 1 teaspoon baking powder
- 1 teaspoon baking soda
- ½ teaspoon salt, optional
- 2 cups whole cranberries, fresh or frozen
- 1 cup walnuts, optional

- Preheat oven to 325 degrees. Grease 2 3 x 7-inch loaf pans.
- With an electric mixer, cream butter and honey. Beat in eggs and orange juice.
- In a separate bowl, stir together whole wheat flour, dry milk powder, baking powder, baking soda and optional salt.
- Gradually blend in flour mixture.
- Stir in cranberries and nuts by hand.
- Turn batter into loaf pans. Bake for 90 minutes or until a toothpick inserted in the center comes out clean.

The Carter House

*T*he Carter House was built in 1906 by Theodore W. Carter. He made his fortune as owner of the nearby Burro Mountain Copper Mine, now known as the Tyrone Mine. In the 1930s and '40s, the building became a clinic for a local doctor who served many of the residents' medical needs. After the clinic, the home returned to private hands. Eventually it was divided into apartments.

After an extensive renovation, Lucy Dilworth opened The Carter House as a Bed & Breakfast on the upper floor, and a 22-bed dormitory-style Hostelling International facility on the lower floor. Lucy had worked for American Youth Hostels in San Francisco for about 10 years. She wanted to move to a smaller community that still offered the cultural diversity she was used to in San Francisco. Silver City charmed her with its mix of interesting people, fresh air and wide-open spaces.

Guests in the inn's four guestrooms and one suite have use of the inn's library and the large wrap-around porch with views of Silver City and mountains beyond. They can begin a walking tour of historic Silver City from that front porch. It was right next door at the Legal Tender Mine where silver was discovered in 1870, resulting in the renaming of the settlement of San Vicente de Cienega as Silver City.

Today, Silver City, elev. 5,900 feet, is the gateway to the Gila Wilderness Area, the oldest designated wilderness in the country, offering wonderful hiking, biking, bird-watching and rock-hounding. The Gila Cliff Dwellings National Monument offers a close look at the ancient Mimbres culture, famous for its black-and-white pottery, on display at local museums. For a day trip, guests head to the catwalk over Whitewater Creek, flowing out of the Mogollon Mountains, or they picnic at City of Rocks State Park for views of geological formations and the desert landscape. Lucy also directs guests to nearby hot springs, a ghost town and on- and off-road bike trails, popular year 'round in the sunny, mild weather.

The Carter House
101 North Cooper Street
Silver City, NM 88061
505-388-5485

Whole-Wheat Pumpkin Bread

Autumn arrives in Silver City with a refreshing gentleness. Days stay warm and sunny, but nights are crisp and cool. Pumpkins in the Carter House garden are harvested and baked into this special bread. The comforting aroma mixes with scents from the town, as residents prepare for winter by roasting chiles and burning juniper in their fireplaces. Makes 2 loaves.

  4 eggs
2½ cups sugar
  1 cup butter or vegetable oil
  ⅓ cup milk
  2 cups pumpkin
  1 teaspoon vanilla extract
3½ cups whole-wheat flour
  2 teaspoons baking soda
1½ teaspoons ginger or pumpkin pie spice
  1 teaspoon baking powder
  ½ teaspoon salt
  ½ cup raisins, optional
  ½ cup chopped walnuts, optional

- Preheat oven to 350 degrees. Grease 2 9 x 5-inch loaf pans.
- With an electric mixer, beat together the eggs, sugar, butter or oil, milk, pumpkin, and vanilla.
- In a separate bowl, stir together the flour, baking soda, ginger or pumpkin pie spice, baking powder, and salt.
- Stir the flour mixture together with the egg mixture. Stir in the raisins and walnuts, if desired.
- Pour batter into pans. Bake for 50 minutes or until a toothpick inserted in the center comes out clean.
- Cool in the pans for 10 minutes before turning out onto racks to cool completely.

Angel Arbor
Bed & Breakfast Inn

*V*eteran Houston Innkeeper Marguerite Swanson, with her husband, Dean, opened Angel Arbor Bed & Breakfast Inn in September 1995 after a busy six-month restoration. Marguerite successfully operated Durham House B&B Inn, just a half-block away, for ten years before "downsizing" to this slightly smaller Georgian-style home. Both homes were once owned by Jay L. Durham, a Houston Heights benefactor. As father of eight, he aspired to acquire a house for each of his children, but he fell short of that goal because of the Great Depression.

Marguerite, a San Antonio native, easily moved into innkeeping as a profession. "I came from a big family and I was used to entertaining, and I just loved the idea of having people in my house all the time," she said. "I never have a day when I wake up and wish I were doing something else." Durham House quickly established a reputation for gracious accommodations and special occasions, such as unique murder mystery dinners, teas, showers, and small private parties.

In order to have more free time, she and Dean bought the elegant red brick residence that is now the Angel Arbor. It has five spacious guestrooms upstairs, three of which have double whirlpool tubs. The 1923 home, built for Katherine and John McTighe, had most recently been used for offices. The Swansons removed glued-down carpet, refinished the original hardwood floors, installed new bathrooms, and replaced many fixtures. They turned the screened porch into a year-round solarium overlooking the garden, with Marguerite's favorite angel statue and Dean's favorite vine-covered arbor. Guests enjoy the garden as well as the first-floor parlor, solarium, sunroom, and dining room. Learn more on the Web, www.angelarbor.com

Angel Arbor Bed & Breakfast Inn

848 Heights Boulevard
Houston, TX 77007
713-868-4654 ■ Toll-free 800-722-8788
Fax 713-861-3189

Yellow Squash Bread

Innkeeper Marguerite Swanson was inspired to make this unusual bread when, after innkeeping for about three years, a guest noticed that far too many B&Bs had a repertoire which included only banana bread or blueberry muffins. Makes 1 loaf.

   2 cups flour
   2 teaspoons baking powder
   1 teaspoon cinnamon
  ½ teaspoon baking soda
  ½ teaspoon salt
  ½ teaspoon ginger
  ¼ teaspoon nutmeg
  ¼ teaspoon ground cloves
   2 eggs
  ¾ cup sugar
  ⅓ cup vegetable oil
  ½ cup sour cream
  ⅓ cup apricot preserves
   2 cups unpeeled and shredded yellow squash

- Preheat oven to 350 degrees. Grease and flour a 9 x 5-inch loaf pan.
- In a large bowl, stir together the flour, cinnamon, baking powder, baking soda, salt, ginger, nutmeg, and cloves.
- In a separate bowl, whisk together the eggs, sugar, oil, sour cream, and pre-serves. Stir in the shredded squash by hand. Gradually add the egg-squash mixture to the flour mixture.
- Pour batter into a pan. Bake for 1 hour, or until a toothpick inserted in the middle comes out clean.

Window on the Winds

*L*eanne McClain's two-story log home is the perfect base for a Wyoming vacation. The second floor, with four guestrooms featuring lodgepole pine beds, is reserved for guests. A view of the Wind River Mountains from the fireside gathering room has been known to take more than one guest's breath away.

Leanne is an archeologist who enjoys sharing her perspective on the area and can offer information about the history of the Green River Basin and the Wind River Range. She is also happy to help guests plan their fishing, rafting, riding, skiing, or hiking adventures.

Window on the Winds is located directly on the Continental Divide Snowmobile Trail at elevation 7,175 feet. A guided inn-to-inn snowmobile tour that leads into Yellowstone National Park leaves right from the property. Guests can snowmobile from the front door, through the Wind River Mountains and on into Yellowstone National Park. Other winter adventures include dog sledding and racing, and both cross-country and downhill skiing.

Whatever the season, guests can return from a day of outdoor adventure to relax and enjoy the hot tub. Fresh fruits, vegetables, and whole grains are always on the breakfast menu. Leanne specializes in western hospitality, even offering to board guests' horses. The bed and breakfast is within a two-hour drive of Jackson Hole and the Grand Teton and Yellowstone National Parks. Learn more on the Web, www.cruising-america.com/windowonwinds

Window on the Winds Bed & Breakfast

10151 Highway 191, P.O. Box 996
Pinedale, WY 82941
307-367-2600
Fax 307-367-2395
Toll-free 888-367-1345

Zucchini Maple Bread

This bread is a popular afternoon snack, welcoming guests back to the inn after a day of outdoor activities. Makes 2 loaves.

         3 eggs
         1 cup sugar
         1 cup brown sugar, packed
         1 cup vegetable oil
    $1\frac{1}{2}$ teaspoons maple flavoring
         2 cups grated zucchini
    $2\frac{1}{2}$ cups flour
    $\frac{1}{2}$ cup wheat germ
         2 teaspoons baking soda
         2 teaspoons salt
    $\frac{1}{2}$ teaspoon baking powder
         1 cup chopped nuts
    $\frac{1}{3}$ cup sesame seeds

- Preheat oven to 350 degrees. Grease and flour two 9 x 5-inch loaf pans.
- With an electric mixer, beat together the eggs, sugar, brown sugar, oil, and maple extract.
- Stir in the zucchini, flour, wheat germ, baking soda, salt, baking powder, and nuts.
- Pour the batter into pans. Sprinkle tops with sesame seeds.
- Bake for 1 hour or until a toothpick inserted in the center comes out clean.

Yankee Hill Inn Bed & Breakfast

The ambiance of quiet, small town life in the heart of the Kettle Moraine recreational area is what Yankee Hill Inn Bed and Breakfast Innkeepers Peg and Jim Stahlman find draws guests to their two historic homes-turned-B&Bs.

Yankee Hill Inn B&B is comprised of two historic homes restored by the Stahlmans. One is a Sheboygan County landmark, a Queen Anne Victorian–style, built in 1891. The other is an 1870 Gothic Italianate listed on the National Register of Historic Places. Both were built in the "Yankee Hill" area of Plymouth by hard-working, affluent brothers, Henry and Gilbert Huson.

Yankee Hill Inn has 12 guestrooms, decorated with period antiques and other touches to reflect historic lodging. Six guestrooms have single whirlpool tubs. Landscaped yards, parlors, fireplaces, and an enclosed front porch allow the guests to gather and relax. Each morning, guests wake up to the aroma of a full breakfast, featuring home-baked muffins and breads, and the cookie jar is open to guests.

From the Inn, guests take a short walk through Huson Park and across the Mullet River footbridge into downtown Plymouth, where they can explore charming antique and gift shops and dine in excellent restaurants. At the Plymouth Center is an art gallery, the Plymouth Historical Museum, and visitor information.

Outdoor adventures surround Plymouth in the glacially sculpted terrain. Enjoy the Kettle Moraine State Forest, many lakes, marked nature trails and the Ice Age Trail for hiking and biking. The paved Old Plank Road recreational trail, historic Plymouth walking tour, Road America race track and the Kohler Design Center, featuring the latest in Kohler bathroom and kitchen ideas, are also popular. Sheboygan and Lake Michigan are just 15 minutes away. Learn more on the Web, www.yankeehillinn.com

Yankee Hill Inn Bed & Breakfast
405 Collins Street
Plymouth, WI 53073
920-892-2222 ■ Fax 920-892-6228

Zucchini Nut Bread

This old favorite, spiked with plenty of cinnamon, has become a standby for busy Innkeeper Peg Stahlman. She's tried other Zucchini Bread recipes, but still comes back to this one! Makes 2 loaves.

   3 **eggs**
1½ **cups sugar**
  ¾ **cup vegetable oil**
  1 **tablespoon vanilla**
  2 **cups flour**
  1   **tablespoon cinnamon**
  1   **teaspoon baking soda**
  1 **teaspoon salt**
  2 **cups coarsely grated, peeled zucchini**
  1 **cup chopped pecans or walnuts**

- Preheat oven to 350 degrees. Grease and flour 2 9 x 5-inch loaf pans.
- With an electric mixer, beat eggs until foamy.
- Beat in sugar, oil and vanilla until thick and lemon colored.
- Beat in flour, cinnamon, baking soda and salt, mixing well.
- Stir in zucchini by hand. Then fold in nuts.
- Turn the batter out into loaf pans and bake for 1 hour and 15 minutes or until a knife inserted in the middle comes out clean.

The Inn on Maple

*T*he Inn on Maple sits below the bluffs of Green Bay, midway up the Door Peninsula. Originally constructed in 1902 as a residence and meat market, the building changed hands many times before its 1983 renovation as an inn. The National Register of Historic Places lists it as one of the finest examples of commercial-residential stovewood buildings in Wisconsin.

Guests at The Inn on Maple enjoy privacy in quiet rooms furnished with antique beds. Breakfast is served on the sunny enclosed front porch or in the Gathering Room and may include fresh fruits, juice, homemade muffins or breads, and special entrées, such as stuffed French toasts, fluffy pancakes, and baked strattas and egg dishes.

Louise and Bill Robbins moved from their suburban Chicago hometown and purchased the Inn in the spring of 1995. They wanted to enjoy and share the beauty of Door County and, in particular, Sister Bay. They have made it their goal to share their enthusiasm for the Door Peninsula with their guests all year 'round.

Sister Bay and the Door Peninsula offer dozens of activities in any season, from sledding, skiing, and snowmobiling to boating, biking, fishing, golfing, and swimming. The Inn is conveniently located near Peninsula State Park, Newport State Park, Birch Creek Music Center, nature sanctuaries, the village beach, restaurants, shops, and a bluffside hiking trail.

The Inn on Maple
414 Maple Drive
Sister Bay, WI 54234
920-854-5107

Zucchini Pineapple Bread

The crushed pineapple is the special ingredient in an already wonderful zucchini bread recipe, said Louise Robbins, innkeeper. "This quick bread has been a favorite in our family for years." Makes 2 loaves.

- 3 eggs
- 1 cup vegetable oil
- 2 cups sugar
- 2 teaspoons vanilla extract
- 3 cups flour
- 2 teaspoons baking soda
- 2 teaspoons cinnamon
- 1 teaspoon nutmeg
- 1 teaspoon salt
- ¼ teaspoon baking powder
- 2 cups unpeeled and shredded zucchini
- 1 cup crushed pineapple, well drained
- 1 cup chopped dates (may substitute raisins)
- 1 cup chopped pecans

- ■ Preheat oven to 350 degrees. Liberally grease 2 9 x 5-inch loaf pans.
- ■ With an electric mixer, beat the eggs, oil, sugar, and vanilla until thick.
- ■ Beat in the flour, baking soda, cinnamon, nutmeg, salt, and baking powder.
- ■ Mix in the zucchini, pineapple, dates, and pecans by hand
- ■ Pour batter into pans. Bake for about 1 hour or until a toothpick inserted in the middle comes out clean.

ARIZONA
The Graham Bed & Breakfast Inn and Adobe Village; Sedona, AZ —
Apricot Banana Bread (19)
White Mountain Lodge; Greer, AZ — *Apple Walnut Bread (15)*

CALIFORNIA
The Blue Spruce Inn; Soquel, CA — *Aunt Nadine's Buttermilk Nut Bread (25)*
Lord Mayor's Bed & Breakfast Inn; Long Beach, CA — *Apple Pecan Bread (13)*

DELAWARE
Wild Swan Inn; Lewes, DE — *Honey Banana Bread (67)*

MAINE
The Bagley House; Durham (Freeport), ME — *Banana Walnut Bread (29)*

MICHIGAN
The Lamplighter Bed & Breakfast; Ludington, MI — *Peach Almond Yogurt Bread
(93)*

MINNESOTA
Martin Oaks Bed & Breakfast; Dundas, MN — *Banana Pecan Bread (27)*
The Stone Hearth Inn; Little Marais, MN — *Orange Pecan Pumpkin Bread (89)*
Thorwood and Rosewood Inns; Hastings, MN — *Garlic Herb Beer Bread (61), Goat
Cheese and Sun-Dried Tomato Flat Bread (63), Raisin Beer Bread (103)*

MISSOURI
The Doanleigh Inn; Kansas City, MO — *Banana White Chocolate Loaf (31), Chocolate
Pepper Pound Cake (43), Pineapple Yogurt Bread (97), Sour Cream Raisin Bread
(111)*

NEW HAMPSHIRE
Apple Gate Bed & Breakfast; Peterborough, NH — *Irish Soda Bread (69),
Orange Apple Tea Bread (85)*
The Inn at Maplewood Farm; Hillsborough, NH — *Grandmother Jeanne's
Banana Nut Bread (65)*
Watch Hill Bed & Breakfast; Center Harbor, NH — *Cheddar Sausage Bread (39),
Creamy Double Corn Bread (53), Savory Christmas Bread (109)*

NEW MEXICO
The Carter House; Silver City, NM — *Whole-Wheat Pumpkin Bread (117)*
Inn on the Rio; Taos, NM — *Breakfast Pear Loaf (33), Easy Applesauce Loaf (57)*

NORTH CAROLINA
Claddagh Inn; Hendersonville, NC — *Strawberry Bread (113)*